healthy eat

pregnancy

D0263010

Erika Lenkert
with Brooke R Alpert MS, RD, CDN

healthy eating during
pregnancy

Photography by Will Heap

Kyle Books

First published in Great Britain in 2011 by
Kyle Books
23 Howland Street, London W1T 4AY
general.enquiries@kyle-cathie.com
www.kylebooks.com

ISBN: 978-1-85626-962-9

A CIP catalogue record for this title is available from the
British Library.

10 9 8 7 6 5 4 3 2 1

Project editor Anja Schmidt
Designer Geoff Hayes
Photographer Will Heap
Food styling Aya Nishimura
Prop styling Wei Tang
Copy editor Jane Tunks
Production by Nic Jones, Sheila Smith and Lisa Pinnell

Colour reproduction by Sang Choy
Printed and bound by Star Standard Industries Pte. Ltd.

Important note
The information and advice contained in this book are intended as a general guide to
healthy eating and are not specific to individuals or their particular circumstances. This
book is not intended to replace treatment by a qualified practitioner. Neither the authors
nor the publishers can be held responsible for claims arising from the inappropriate
use of any dietary regime. Do not attempt self-diagnosis or self-treatment for serious or
long-term conditions without consulting a medical professional or qualified practitioner.

contents

foreword

By improving maternal health, we could give our children a better start in life, reduce infant mortality and the numbers of low-birth weight babies – this is the view of the UK Government and is shared by health professionals worldwide.

One of the most important things you can do for your baby is to have a healthy diet (and lifestyle) both prior to getting pregnant and during the pregnancy itself.

Not all pregnancies are planned, some are delightful surprises, but if you are planning a pregnancy there are many things to consider. Eating well, maintaining a healthy weight and getting enough of the important nutrients, will benefit you and your baby. Once the baby is on the way you may only need to make a few changes if you are already eating a healthy diet. Even if you are not, it isn't too late to start – even if you are several months pregnant. Changing to a better diet now will help your body cope with the remainder of your pregnancy and the demands of breastfeeding, as well as being of benefit to your developing baby, to give them a good start in life and a good foundation for long-term health.

If you have particular dietary concerns then you are best to talk it over with your Doctor or Midwife but this book will be a great way to enjoy eating during your pregnancy and knowing that you are staying healthy at the same time.

Liz Campbell

Liz Campbell
Director of Wellbeing of Women

**WELLBEING
OF WOMEN**

introduction

If you have this book in your hands, congratulations! Not only are you pregnant, but you are also doing one of the smartest things you can do to ensure the health and happiness of you and your unborn baby. Why? Because, as you've probably already discovered, pregnancy comes with a cornucopia of dietary conundrums, from what you should or shouldn't eat to how much weight you should or shouldn't gain, to how on earth you can possibly stay on track when your cravings are strong enough to make you consider breaking into a bakery after hours. Add to that the litany of boring pregnancy-food recommendations out there (tofu nut loaf, anyone?), and it's enough to make even the nutrition-conscious mum-to-be shrug her shoulders and dive into a tub of ice cream.

That's where this book comes in. The following introductory information, provided by the fabulous nutritionist and mother Brooke R Alpert, answers all your nutrition questions and provides concrete guidelines for smart eating for all nine months. Then I follow up with 100 spectacularly delicious, even downright indulgent, recipes that make eating for optimum baby and mummy health a truly satisfying experience. Collected from some of the world's finest chefs and my own kitchen, these fast and easy-to-prepare dishes will be useful for years to come, especially once your little one starts to move past baby rice.

So don't be afraid to cater to your newly gargantuan appetite, even if it's peppered with bouts of nausea (hey, we've got food for that!). With these recipes, you can actually have your cake and eat it too.

Just remember to eat three small meals a day and two snacks, which will help ward off hunger attacks and keep your body energised for the miraculous task at hand, supplement with prenatal vitamins as directed and enjoy a variety of foods, ensuring that you get a wide range of essential nutrients. Beyond that, just savour this time – literally and figuratively. With all the hard work your body is doing, you absolutely deserve it.

Warmest regards to you and your growing family,

Erika Lenkert

eating for two

Though we'd all like to believe that 'eating for two' literally means doubling up on calories and dessert helpings, that's not actually the case. Here's why: the average woman needs to consume between 1,800 and 2,200 calories per day to keep her engine running smoothly and efficiently. Very active women and teenagers may need as many as 2,900 calories per day, and in those cases they should ask their midwife or doctors for caloric guidance.

During the first trimester, the baby's developmental focus is on the brain and doesn't require too many extra calories at this stage. Furthermore, recent guidelines in the UK advise that even during the third trimester, when your baby is seriously bulking up, only about 200 extra calories are required – for example, a slice of toast with baked beans or a bowl of whole-grain cereal with semi-skimmed milk (NHS Choices 2009a).

On the bright side, it is highly recommended that you eat five – you heard us, five! – times each day. While we're not talking heaped platefuls of food, calorie-minded guidelines offer plenty of room for dining pleasure, as evidenced by the sample diet plan on page 10. Eating frequent portion-controlled meals and snacks ensures that you don't become overly famished and your developing baby gets a steady flow of much-needed nutrients.

what to gain?

The optimum amount of weight to gain during pregnancy depends on how much you weighed prior to becoming pregnant as well as how many children you are carrying at one time. There are no official guidelines for weight gain in pregnancy in the UK, there is only the general advice that you should put on somewhere between 10kg and 12.5kg. In the USA, pregnancy weight-gain recommendations are more wide-ranging and give detailed advice for gestational weight gain for underweight, normal weight and overweight women. You might find it helpful to follow the American advice and it certainly won't do you any harm.

A woman at a 'healthy' pre-pregnancy weight, as determined by the body mass index (BMI) chart opposite,
should gain approximately 11.3–15.9kg during her three trimesters carrying a single baby. Targets for women who are 'overweight' are 6.8–11.3kg, and it's recommended that women who fall into the 'obese' or 'extremely obese' category should try to gain no more than 5–9kg. 'Underweight' women should aim for 12.7–18kg to prevent having a low birth-weight baby.

Women with a 'healthy' BMI who are expecting twins or triplets will need to gain approximately 15.9–20.4kg. There is unfortunately not enough information for women expecting three or more babies, but significant weight should be gained, approximately 0.9kg per week, during the second and third trimesters.

when to gain?

Regardless of your pre-pregnancy weight, there are some healthy weight-gain guidelines that are ideal for ensuring that you are getting enough, but not too much, caloric energy. Do, however, keep in mind that these are only guidelines and that each pregnancy is unique; in fact, weight changes may even vary for the same woman from pregnancy to pregnancy:

During the first trimester, a weight gain of 0.45–0.68kg per month is considered normal. However, women suffering from severe morning sickness or even all-day sickness may actually lose a slight amount of weight during this time. (And conversely, women who are indulging as if every meal is their last will gain more.) Since every woman is different, it's not critical to be right on target here, but it is important to contact your doctor if you are having a hard time keeping food or water down, as you may be suffering from hyperemesis gravidarum, which is a severe form of morning sickness that needs to be monitored closely. See Morning Sickness (page 23) for more on this.

During the second and third trimesters, your weight gain will begin to pick up to about 0.23–0.45kg per week. Some months you may gain more, some less, which is normal with all the hormonal and physical changes happening (think breasts enlarging as they prepare for milk production, your uterus expanding, the placenta growing and your baby developing). For some women, weight gain slows down during the last few weeks of pregnancy, even as your baby continues to grow because, as your body prepares for labour, it holds on to fewer fluids. And if that nesting instinct kicks in, women tend to burn extra calories as they prepare for the baby's arrival.

BMI chart

Weight lbs		100	105	110	115	120	125	130	135	140	145	150	155	160	165	170	175	180	185	190	195	200	205	210	215
	kgs	45.5	45.7	50.0	52.3	54.5	56.8	59.1	61.4	63.6	65.9	68.2	70.5	72.7	75.0	77.3	79.5	81.8	84.1	86.4	88.6	90.9	93.2	95.5	97.7
Height in/cm		Underweight				Healthy						Overweight					Obese					Extremely Obese			
5'00"	152.4	19	20	21	22	23	24	25	26	27	28	29	30	31	32	33	34	35	36	37	38	39	40	41	42
5'1"	154.9	18	19	20	21	22	23	24	25	26	27	28	29	30	31	32	33	34	35	36	36	37	38	39	40
5'2"	157.4	18	19	20	21	22	22	23	24	25	26	27	28	29	30	31	32	33	33	34	35	36	37	38	39
5'3"	160.0	17	18	19	20	21	22	23	24	24	25	26	27	28	29	30	31	32	32	33	34	35	36	37	38
5'4"	162.5	17	18	18	19	20	21	22	23	24	24	25	26	27	28	29	30	31	31	32	33	34	35	36	37
5'5"	165.1	16	17	18	19	20	20	21	22	23	24	25	25	26	27	28	29	30	30	31	32	33	34	35	35
5'6"	167.6	16	17	17	18	19	20	21	21	22	23	24	25	25	26	27	28	29	29	30	31	32	33	34	34
5'7"	170.1	15	16	17	18	18	19	20	21	22	22	23	24	25	25	26	27	28	29	29	30	31	32	33	33
5'8"	172.1	15	16	16	17	18	19	19	20	21	22	22	23	24	25	25	26	27	28	28	29	30	31	32	32
5'9"	175.2	14	15	16	17	17	18	19	20	20	21	22	22	23	24	25	25	26	27	28	28	29	30	31	31
5'10"	177.8	14	15	15	16	17	18	18	19	20	20	21	22	23	23	24	25	25	26	27	28	28	29	30	30
5'11"	180.3	14	14	15	16	16	17	18	18	19	20	21	21	22	23	23	24	25	25	26	27	28	28	29	30
6'0"	182.8	13	14	14	15	16	17	17	18	19	19	20	21	21	22	23	23	24	25	25	26	27	27	28	29
		13	13	14	15	15	16	17	17	18	19	19	20	21	21	22	23	23	24	25	25	26	27	27	28
		12	13	14	14	15	16	17	17	18	18	19	19	20	21	21	22	23	23	24	25	25	26	27	27
6'3"	190.5	12	13	13	14	15	15	16	16	17	18	18	19	20	20	21	21	22	23	23	24	25	25	26	26
6'4"	193.0	12	12	13	14	14	15	15	16	17	17	18	18	19	20	20	21	22	22	23	23	24	25	25	26

where the weight goes

Come birth day, you might be surprised to find that your baby weighs only 3.2kg, when you've packed on enough weight to represent five healthy children. Fortunately, the added weight is not simply new appendages to your thighs, hips or belly. Between the baby, placenta, amniotic fluid and breasts, the numbers add up quickly. Alas, beyond bloating from water retention, most additional kilos acquired during pregnancy are mementos of overindulgence. They are also yours to keep – and lose – after your baby is born.

Average weight breakdown

Where	How much?
Baby	2.7–4.5kg
Placenta	0.45–0.9kg
Amniotic fluid	0.9kg
Breasts	0.45kg
Uterus	0.9kg
Increase in blood volume	1.4kg
Body fat	2.3 or more kg
Increased muscle tissue and fluid	1.8–3.2kg
Total	**At least 11.3kg**

why how much you gain matters

There is more to monitoring weight gain than whether or not you will fit into your favourite jeans after pregnancy. Gaining too much can heighten your risk of gestational diabetes (high blood sugar levels brought on by pregnancy), lead to a larger (and thus harder to deliver) baby, and can heighten the risk of your baby being an overweight or obese child and adult.

On the flip side, eating enough or even a bit too much helps ensure that your infant will be born at the desirable weight of more than 2.6kg, which lowers the chances of heart and lung disease, diabetes, hypertension and hypoglycaemia developing later in life and the likelihood of a low Apgar score (a test to determine an infant's physical condition) at birth.

how many calories a day?

Recommendations for daily calorie intake do vary and while guidelines in the UK advise you don't go beyond 2,000 calories a day, Australia and the US allow an extra 500 calories on top of that. But if all this talk of caloric monitoring makes you think you're in for a bland, restrictive dining experience for the next nine months, check out this chart highlighting a single day's menu possibilities, complete with recipes from this book.

Meal	Calories
Breakfast	
Courgette Frittata	164
Two slices wholemeal toast	180
Decaf skimmed latte (225g)	70
Snack	
Cucumber and Mint Sandwich	90
Fat-free vanilla yogurt (175g)	130
Lunch	
Decadent Chicken Soup	135
Watermelon, Rocket and Feta Salad	104
Wholemeal pitta bread (small)	80
Snack	
Parmesan-Dusted Kale Crisps	90
Ginger Limeade	44
Dinner	
Red Snapper with Vinaigrette Provençal	380
Oven-Roasted Parmesan Fries	376
Chinese-Style Green Beans	63
Dessert	
Chocolate Coconut Oatmeal Cookie	120
Skimmed milk (245g)	90
Total	**1,899**

noshing for optimum nutrients

Surely you know that it's not just how much you eat, but what you eat that matters when you're growing a baby. Still, knowing how to identify and consume the most helpful nutrients can be a challenge even to the healthiest mums-to-be. These primers will help you bite through befuddlement and get to the meat of the matter.

macronutrients

All the energy you need for pregnancy comes from your diet – specifically carbohydrates, protein and fat. Together with fibre, the following are the four macronutrients necessary for a healthy pregnancy.

carbohydrates

Carbohydrates are a great source of energy for your pregnant body because, of all the possible calorie sources, your body burns them the most quickly and efficiently. The energy supplied by carbohydrates is needed for both you and your baby's brains, muscles and central nervous systems. Without enough daily carbohydrates, your body will turn to protein for energy instead of using it for the important growth functions for your changing body and especially for your growing baby. (For more on protein, see page 14.) As a result, carbohydrates should make up a significant amount of your daily calories. (Need an excuse to indulge in pasta? Now you have it!)

Simple carbohydrates versus complex carbohydrates
Not all carbs are created equal. 'Simple' and 'complex' carbohydrates have different benefits and, in the case of simple carbs, potential drawbacks.

Simple carbohydrates – found in fruit, milk and even some vegetables – provide plenty of healthy nutrients, vitamins, minerals and fibre in addition to energy and are broken down quickly by the body. But they are also found in the form of refined sugars and processed foods, such as fizzy drinks, biscuits, cake and confectionery. These types of simple carbs contain 'empty calories', meaning they have no nutritional benefit. Eating too much of them can lead to excessive weight gain, high blood sugar and even gestational diabetes.

Complex carbohydrates – found in whole grains, root vegetables, beans and more – contain B vitamins, which aid in the growth and development of your baby. They also contain magnesium, a mineral that helps relax the uterine muscular lining and build bones and regulate nerves for you and your baby. They also contain trace minerals, such as copper, which aid in the formation of connective tissue. Needless to say, complex carbs are very good for you and your little one.

Good carbohydrate choices	Carbohydrates to avoid or eat sparingly
Whole grains	Granulated sugar
Wholemeal bread	Cakes
Potatoes	Biscuits
Sweet potatoes	Muffins
Beans and other legumes	Pastries
Low-fat dairy	Confectionery
Fruit	Fizzy drinks
Barley	
Couscous	
Quinoa	
Brown rice	
Multigrain cereal	

fat

Contrary to what we are regularly told, fat has a lot of important beneficial qualities, especially for pregnant women. An essential nutrient, it helps support the growth of the placenta and other tissues, helps develop your baby's brain and central nervous system, prevents pre-term delivery and low birth weight, and transports vitamins A, D, E and K from you to your growing baby. Plus, with the highest amount of calories per gram compared to other nutrients, fat aids in providing enough calories to ensure your body has the stamina to grow your baby and keep you energised along the way.

Add to that the fact that essential fatty acids during pregnancy and lactation have been linked to babies with higher intelligence, better vision and more mature central nervous systems, and you've got all the reason you need to welcome fat as up to 30 per cent of your daily caloric intake.

That said, all fat is not created equal. There are four kinds of fats found in food: monounsaturated, polyunsaturated, saturated and hydrogenated, and some are better for you than others.

The good
Monounsaturated fat (found in olives and avocados): Considered a good fat because it has a healthy effect on blood cholesterol levels.

Polyunsaturated fat (found in vegetable oils, nuts and seeds): Contains the good fatty acids omega-3 and omega-6, which are crucial for your baby's development.

The bad
Saturated fat (found in red meat, full-fat dairy and butter): Considered bad because it may increase cholesterol.

Hydrogenated fat (also known as trans fat and primarily found in processed foods): Used to extend shelf life of packaged foods, and can increase your risk of heart disease.

Omega-3 fats

Docosahexanoic Acid (DHA) and Eicosapentanoic Acid (EPA) are the long chain polyunsaturated (LCP) omega-3 fats that are vital for brain growth, visual and neurological development in the foetus and young infant. Women who do not eat fish may not get enough of these fats. The International Society for the Study of Fatty Acids and Lipids recommends that pregnant women should consume 200mg DHA/day as is recommended for the general adult population. A minimum total intake of 500mg of DHA and EPA is also recommended. This can be achieved by eating one or two portions of oily fish a week. A portion is about 100g cooked weight.

During pregnancy oily fish intake should be limited to 2 servings per week. Pregnant women who do not eat oily fish may choose to take supplements of omega-3 fats as studies have shown that supplements containing 200mg – 1g DHA/day; and 500mg – 2.7g in total of omega-3 LCPs (DHA and EPA) provide a useful daily intake and have not caused harm in pregnant women.

protein

Protein is absolutely critical for pregnant women because it is used to make new cells, manufacture enzymes and hormones and control fluid balance, which directly affects blood pressure. During pregnancy, more than 25 per cent of all the protein you eat goes directly to the baby, placenta and uterine lining. It also acts as a much-needed energy supply if you don't eat enough carbohydrates.

For the first trimester, your protein intake needn't vary from your pre-pregnant days and having huge amounts of extra protein in pregnancy should be discouraged. It's during the second and third trimester, when the baby undergoes the most rapid growth, that your protein requirements increase slightly. Meeting these needs is very doable – even for women with food aversions or morning sickness, or vegetarian or vegan lifestyles – because protein is present in an amazing array of foods, including grains, nuts and beans.

There's an extra perk in eating protein: many foods that contain it also include other important nutritional powerhouses. For example, lean red meat, chicken and seafood are all great sources of iron as well as protein. Milk, another protein provider, also has vitamin D and calcium, which are important components for bone development.

Alas, some proteins can be high in saturated fats (ice cream, steaks and chicken skin), so try to avoid mixing the bad with the good by choosing lean meats, skinless poultry and low-fat or fat-free dairy. But note that in many low-fat dairy foods, vitamins A and D are also removed so check that they are added back in the low-fat products that you buy.

List of protein-rich foods

Food	Serving size	Protein (grams)
Beef, extra lean, cooked	85g	25
Bread, wholemeal	1 slice	3
Bulgar wheat, cooked	182g	6
Cereal, bran flakes	30g	3
Cheddar	25g	7
Chicken, dark meat	85g	23
Chicken, white meat	85g	27
Chickpeas, cooked	164g	18
Cottage cheese, low-fat	225g	28
Egg	1 large	6
Egg white	1 large	3
Lentils, cooked	198g	17
Milk, full-fat or skimmed	225g	8
Mozzarella, reduced-fat	25g	7
Peanut butter	2 tablespoons	9
Pork tenderloin, cooked	85g	26
Salmon, cooked	85g	22
Tofu, raw	124g	10
Wheat germ	29g	7
Yogurt, fat-free fruit	82g	7
Yogurt, Greek	245g	20

fibre

Fibre is a cholesterol-reducing component of plant foods that is found in whole grains, vegetables, fruits, legumes, nuts and seeds. For pregnant women, one of fibre's best benefits is that it can relieve constipation and haemorrhoids (common pregnancy side effects) because it softens and stimulates stools, and allows them to be passed more easily.

An important partner to fibre is fluid. Fibre absorbs a significant amount of fluid while travelling through your digestive tract, so it's important to be properly hydrated in order to benefit from fibre as much as possible (see Hydration on page 22 for more information).

A good amount of fibre to aim for every day is 20–35g. See the chart below to find out how much fibre is in your healthy food choices.

Fibre-rich foods

Food	Serving size	Total fibre (grams)*
Fruit		
Apple	1 medium	4.4
Banana	1 medium	3.1
Figs, dried	2 medium	1.6
Orange	1 medium	3.1
Pear	1 medium	5.5
Raisins	2 tablespoons	1.0
Raspberries	123g	8.0
Strawberries	175g	3.8

Food	Serving size	Total fibre (grams)*
Grains, cereal & pasta		
Pearl barley, cooked	160g	6.0
Bran flakes	30g	5.3
Bread, rye	1 slice	1.9
Bread, wholemeal or multigrain	1 slice	1.9
Brown rice, cooked	195g	3.5
Oat bran muffin	1 medium	5.2
Oatmeal, cooked	234g	4.0
Popcorn, air-popped	24g	3.5
Spaghetti, wholemeal, cooked	140g	6.2
Legumes, nuts & seeds		
Almonds	28.4g (23 nuts)	3.5
Baked beans, vegetarian cooked	253g	10.4
Black beans, cooked	172g	15.0
Lentils, cooked	198g	15.6
Lima beans, cooked	188g	13.2
Pecan nuts	28.4g (19 halves)	2.7
Pistachio nuts	28.4g (49 nuts)	2.9
Split peas, cooked	196g	16.3
Sunflower seed kernels	36g	3.9
Vegetables		
Carrot, raw	1 medium	1.7
Broccoli, boiled	156g	5.1
Brussels sprouts, cooked	156g	4.1
Globe artichoke, cooked	1 medium	10.3
Peas, cooked	160g	8.8
Potato, baked	1 medium	2.9
Savoy cabbage, cooked	145g	4.1
Sweetcorn, cooked	164g	4.2
Tomato purée	63g	2.7

micronutrients

As the name suggests, these nutrients are little guys compared with the 'macro' carbohydrates, fat, protein and fibre. But that doesn't mean they are any less significant. Vitamins, which are technically micronutrients, control your digestive system and the metabolism and absorption of carbohydrates, protein and fat. Below are descriptions of the micronutrients that are especially beneficial to you right now.

calcium

Calcium plays a large role in female and foetus health. Circulating through your bloodstream, it is critical for cellular functioning, nerve transmissions and a healthy heartbeat. Stored in your bones and your body, it is tapped to help build your baby's bones and teeth.

Luckily, your body is incredibly smart and once it recognises that your baby is using up your stored calcium supply, your hormone levels change to allow for more calcium absorption from the foods you eat. This system is so efficient that while pregnant, you may absorb twice as much calcium as you did before pregnancy. However, even heightened absorption doesn't promise you will get enough calcium. For that reason, in the UK, it's recommended that pregnant and breastfeeding women get 750 to 1,500 milligrams of calcium a day. Many pregnant women take prenatal supplements, which contain calcium, but it's still very important to get enough calcium in your diet.

Dairy products are great sources of calcium and they contain protein and vitamin D, which also benefit pregnant women. If you are lactose intolerant or a vegetarian, there are many plant foods that are a good source of calcium, though be aware that there are some that also contain phytic acid or oxalic acid, which can interfere with the body's ability to absorb the nutrient. Spinach, sweet potatoes, rhubarb and green beans are all high in oxalic acid, while wholegrain bread, beans, seeds, nuts, grains and soy products all contain phytic acid. To be certain that you get enough, look for calcium-fortified foods.

Calcium-rich foods

Food	Serving size	Calcium (mg)
Dairy products		
Cheese, cottage cheese	113g	75mg
Cheese, Gruyère	28.4g	287
Ice cream	72g	85
Mozzarella cheese, fat-reduced	28.4g	185
Milk (all types)	245g	300
Non-dairy products:		
Broccoli, cooked	78g	45
Okra, cooked	80g	50
Orange	1 medium	50
Orange juice (fortified)	186g	225
Salmon, canned	85g	205
Soya milk (fortified)	245g	250–300
Tofu (fortified)	124g	260
White flour products	2 slices white bread	72

B vitamins

These vitamins, which help your body release and use energy from the food it digests, are critical during pregnancy. Fortunately, they are easy to come by as they are found in most food groups, and particularly in leafy green vegetables. However as different types of B vitamins perform different functions, it's important to vary your intake. For example, thiamine, which is found in pork, wholegrains and enriched grain products, helps release energy from carbohydrates. Riboflavin, found in dairy products, offal and enriched grains, helps your body produce that energy. Niacin works on your general metabolism and is found in meat, poultry and seafood, while B6 vitamins help create cells from protein and are found in poultry, fish, pork and bananas. B12, which is found primarily in animal products as well as some fortified foods such as soya milk or cereal, aids in the production of red blood cells and also enables the body to utilise energy from fat and carbohydrates.

Another B vitamin, folate or folic acid, is so important for general health as well as pregnancy that in many countries such as the USA, Canada, Australia and New Zealand it is mandated that many foods are fortified with it. However, that is not the case in the UK where it is added to only a very few brands of bread and breakfast cereals. Folate is responsible for producing and creating new red blood cells. A deficiency can lead anyone to a blood disorder called megaloblastic anemia, while a deficiency around the time of conception and during the first trimester, can result in a baby with neural tube defects (NTDs), including serious birth defects such as spina bifida and anencephaly. Studies have shown that if all women consumed the recommended amounts of folate before and during early pregnancy, up to 70 per cent of all NTDs would be prevented.

Folate is found naturally in foods, and folic acid is a form of folate used in fortified foods and supplements. The folate content of food decreases with long storage times and heat and cooking may also cause a considerable reduction. In the UK it is recommended that all women of child-bearing age get at least 200 micrograms of folate or folic acid a day either from food (fortified or natural) and/or supplements. Pregnant women should aim for at least 300 micrograms per day as soon as they know they are pregnant, with an additional 400 micrograms recommended during the first trimester. Some women, such as those with diabetes, epilepsy, obesity or a family history of having a NTD affected pregnancy, should be advised to take a much higher 5mg daily folic acid supplement.

Fortified folic acid food	Serving size	Folic acid (mcg)
Bread	1 slice	40
Breakfast cereal	30g	100–400
Oatmeal, instant*	117g	80
Pasta, cooked*	70g	100–120
Rice, cooked*	80g	60

* fortified in Australia, not in UK

Naturally occurring folate food	Serving size	Folate (mcg)
Chickpeas, cooked	164g	160
Lentils, cooked	198g	358
Peas, cooked	160g	101
Spinach, cooked	180g	263
Strawberries	140g	26

iron

Your growing baby needs a lot of oxygen to develop and iron is responsible for making haemoglobin, which is the protein in your red blood cells that carries oxygen to your baby. Iron is also a component of myoglobin, a protein that supplies oxygen to your muscles for collagen, a protein in bone, cartilage and connective tissues as well as many enzymes. Finally, as if iron weren't enough of a nutritional superhero already, it also helps you maintain a healthy immune system.

In the UK, women with good iron status prior to conception and who eat a healthy balanced diet are not advised to have extra iron during pregnancy because the rising demands of iron by the growing foetus can be met by diminished losses from the mother (because menstrual bleeding is absent) and increased intestinal iron absorption during pregnancy. The level of absorption increases as pregnancy advances and a greater percentage increase will occur in anaemic than in non-anaemic women. The foetus lays down most of its iron during the last trimester, preparing for the first six months of life. These are usually met at the expense of maternal stores.

However, many UK pregnant women experience iron-deficiency anaemia and are advised to take supplements. Unfortunately, supplements often cause constipation, nausea or both, so it's important to eat foods that are naturally high in iron too. The iron in red meat and oily fish (haem iron) is absorbed better than iron from plant foods (non haem iron).

Women following a no-meat or low-meat diet can increase their iron absorption from cereal and vegetable sources by combining it with vitamin C (e.g. beans on toast with orange juice) and by avoiding drinking tea at mealtimes as the tannins present in tea bind with the iron, reducing its absorption.

Iron-rich foods	Portion size	Iron (mg)
Haeme		
Beef, fillet, cooked	85g	3.1
Beef, sirloin, cooked	85g	2.9
Chicken, skinless breast, or dark meat, cooked	85g	1.0
Tuna, canned	85g	1.3
Prawns, cooked	85g	2.6
Pork, lean, cooked	85g	1.0
Non-haeme		
Fortified breakfast cereal	20g	2–9*
Spinach, boiled	90g	3.2
Potato, baked	1 medium	2.8
Enriched rice, cooked	80g	1.2
Raisins	48g	1.1
Kidney beans, cooked	88g	2.6
Wholemeal bread	1 slice	0.9
Pumpkin seeds	16g	4.2
Lentils, cooked	198g	6.6
Prune juice	256g	3.0

*Can vary depending on brand and size

sodium

Salt is also called sodium chloride and food labels sometimes list salt as sodium. However, there is a simple way to work out how much salt you are eating from the sodium figure: Salt = sodium x 2.5. In the UK, adults, including pregnant women, should eat no more than 6g of salt a day: that's around one full teaspoon. Of course, one easy way to eat less salt is to stop adding extra salt to your food during cooking and at the dinner table, and if you regularly add

salt to food, try cutting it out. To really cut down, you need to become aware of the salt that is already in the food you buy and avoid foods that contain a high amount.

Fortunately, food labels now make this a lot easier. Nutritional information labels are usually on the back of the food packaging. Look at the figure for salt per 100g. High is more than 1.5g salt per 100g (or 0.6g sodium). Low is 0.3g salt or less per 100g (or 0.1g sodium). If the amount of salt per 100g is in between these figures, that is a medium level of salt. As a rule, aim for foods that have a low or medium salt content. Leave high-salt foods for occasional use.

Sodium-rich foods	Portion	Sodium (mg)
Cheese pizza	1 slice	550
Chicken Caesar salad	1 order	1,170
Salt	1 teaspoon	2,300
Soy sauce	1 tablespoon	1,030
Tomato juice	243g	875

vitamin A

This fat-soluble vitamin can be found in both animal and plant foods in different forms. Retinol is a kind of pre-formed vitamin A that's found in animal products. Carotenoids are found in fruits and vegetables and get converted into vitamin A in the body. Milk products are also often fortified with vitamin A.

Vitamin A aids in vision, cell production and immune system health, plus it also aids post-partum tissue repair. Excessive intake of retinol is toxic to the foetus and may cause birth defects but overdosing is nothing to worry about so long as your supplements are in check. To keep retinol intakes to a safe level, avoid liver and foods containing liver and supplements containing the retinol form of vitamin A (e.g. that provide more than 3500mg retinol per day). Retinol is also found in much smaller quantities in nutritious foods such as dairy products and do not need to be avoided.

vitamin K

Since the 1960's, in the UK, throughout Europe and the US, vitamin K has been given to newborns as a single injection just after birth in order to prevent a rare disease called Vitamin K deficiency bleeding. This takes care of all the baby's vitamin K requirements.

vitamin D

The main role of vitamin D is to help your body absorb calcium from food and deposit it into your bones. It is also critical for the development of your baby's teeth and bones. The main source of vitamin D is sunlight when outdoors but at UK latitudes, skin synthesis only occurs during April – September. Only oily fish is a good source of dietary vitamin D but small amounts are provided in fortified fat spreads and there are minimal amounts in meat and eggs. One in four women of childbearing age in the UK has low vitamin D levels. This rises to 1 in 2 women with dark skins who require more exposure to sunlight to make the same amount of vitamin D in their skin.

Natural sources of vitamin D	Fortified vitamin D
Mushrooms	Orange juice
Salmon	Milk
Sardines	Yogurt
Egg	Ready-to-eat cereal
Cheese	Margarine
Liver	

Babies born to women with low vitamin D levels are at higher risk of hypocalcaemic fits and rickets and as both these preventable diseases are on the rise again, women in the UK are advised to take a 10 microgram supplement during pregnancy.

vitamin C

Vitamin C may be best known for its cold-fighting abilities, but it also helps in the production of collagen (helping your skin retain its elasticity), the formation and repair of red blood cells and efficient iron absorption – all of which you especially need now.

Vitamin C-rich foods

Orange	Strawberries
Red pepper	Grapefruit
Kiwi fruit	Lemon
Tomato	Lime

Since it's water-soluble, it can't be stored in the body, which means that you need to reach your vitamin C requirements of 70 milligrams every day. Just one red pepper a day is actually enough to meet your vitamin C minimum.

antioxidants

Antioxidants protect you and your baby's tissues from harmful free radicals (which react with body tissues and damage healthy cells) and reduce the risk to your baby's DNA. Spices such as cinnamon, paprika and ginger are all great sources of antioxidants, as are herbs such as sage, peppermint, oregano, parsley, basil and tarragon, and foods such as dried fruits, nuts and deeply pigmented fruits and vegetables.

hydration

Staying hydrated is extremely important as proper hydration allows your body to perform critical everyday functions, including regulating your body temperature, transporting and distributing nutrients to areas that need them and helping to dispose of waste that, if stored in the body, can create illness. When you're pregnant, drinking enough water is even more essential, as it ensures your body can properly cushion and protect your growing baby. It also aids in the production of your increased blood supply.

To make sure you are properly hydrated, drink at least 3 to 4 pints of water or other hydrating fluids each day. Make sure you space them out throughout the day, and add a few extra glasses while you're at it – your body will thank you for it. Drinking liquids isn't the only way to increase your fluid intake as most fruits and vegetables contain ample amounts of water. However, consider this a bonus and not as a substitute for the 8 glasses of water a day.

Drinks containing caffeine such as caffeinated tea and coffee, cola and some 'energy drinks' should be limited (see page 24). Additional sugary fizzy drinks should also be consumed sparingly, as they can increase your blood sugar too quickly, cause you to put on too much weight and do not provide any nutrients. Juice is a healthy choice but it should be enjoyed in moderation to avoid excessive weight gain.

food cravings

Many expectant mums experience cravings at some point during their pregnancy. While it's a common belief that pregnancy leads you to crave some of the more bizarre food combinations, like pickled onions and ice cream, it may come as a surprise to learn that some of the most popular foods craved are fresh fruit and dairy products.

Food cravings in themselves are not a problem as long as your overall diet remains balanced with foods from all the different food groups, including fruit and vegetables, bread and pasta, meat and fish or vegetarian alternatives like beans, eggs, lentils or soya products and dairy foods. Small amounts of fatty and sugary foods can also be included in a healthy diet (see www.eatwell.gov.uk for more information.

morning sickness

Any pregnant woman with this condition will tell you that 'morning sickness' is a misnomer. Nausea can be a constant and very unwelcome companion at any time of the day or night, and studies show that up to 70 per cent of women suffer from nausea, vomiting or both at sometime during pregnancy. For most women, the queasy feeling begins early in pregnancy, often as one of the first clues to her new condition, and tends to dissipate early in the second trimester, although it can last much longer, even straight through to delivery. No one is really sure why nausea occurs but it's likely that it's due to hormonal changes. There's no 'best' way to quell morning sickness as every woman reacts differently to the popular solutions listed below, but they are all worth trying.

1 Get up slowly in the morning and nibble on some plain crackers before getting out of bed.

2 Avoid nausea triggers. Certain smells or foods may be triggers for you, so avoid them as much as possible.

3 Eat snacks and light meals. Simple, plain foods like crackers can be really helpful when those nauseous waves first come on.

4 Eat small, frequent meals. An empty stomach can be extra-acidic, which can lead to extra heartburn or nausea. Overeating can also lead to discomfort.

5 Drink enough fluids. Dehydration can worsen your nausea; take small sips of water all day long to stay properly hydrated, and don't get overheated.

6 Eat cold meals rather than hot meals because cold meals do not give off the smell that may provoke nausea.

7 Rest up! Nausea and fatigue often go hand in hand, so be sure to get enough sleep.

There is some evidence that ginger and a form of acupuncture, known as acupressure may help to reduce pregnancy nausea in some women.

food-related pregnancy discomforts

Constipation
Pregnancy slows down the movement of food through your digestive tract and can cause constipation, as can the iron supplements you're taking. Increase your dried fruit, fresh fruit and vegetable intake for an increase in fibre and aim for at least six to eight glasses of water a day.

Diarrhoea
Diarrhoea is sometimes caused by hormonal changes, lactose intolerance or sensitivities to certain foods. To combat it, eat more foods that help absorb excess water; bananas, rice, apple sauce and bread and drink a lot of water.

Heartburn
Heartburn is common at the beginning due to the hormonal changes that slow down your digestive system. Later, with a growing baby, crowding causes stomach acid to back up into the oesophagus. To avoid it, eat small, frequent meals, try drinking milk before eating and limit caffeine.

Water retention
Those hormones again – or too much salt in your diet. To quell it, increase your water intake and put your feet up. Eat plenty of water-rich fresh fruits and vegetables. See your doctor if the swelling increases rapidly or causes any discomfort because such symptoms can be associated with pre-eclampsia.

Call your midwife or doctor if you experience uncontrolled vomiting, or are becoming dehydrated as you may be experiencing hyperemesis gravidarum and will need to be closely monitored or hospitalised. Hyperemesis gravidarum affects between 0.3% and 2% of all pregnant women and is the most severe form of nausea and vomiting in pregnancy and is defined as persistent nausea and vomiting leading to dehydration, ketonuria, electrolyte imbalance and weight loss greater than 5% of pre-pregnancy weight.

foods to avoid

There are some foods you shouldn't eat when you're pregnant to avoid exposing yourself to the risk of food poisoning or because they're potentially harmful to your unborn baby.

Alcohol

While guidelines differ slightly throughout the world, the safest bet is to avoid alcohol during your pregnancy, especially because there is really no amount of alcohol that has been proven safe to drink. If you indulged with abandon before you knew you were pregnant, it's not worth stressing over. There's nothing you can do about it now, and plenty of women before you have done the same and gone on to have healthy children.

Still, it's a proven fact that excessive alcohol consumption during pregnancy can lead to fetal alcohol syndrome, which encompasses a collection of mental and physical problems in your baby, as well as other developmental disorders. However, if you do decide to drink alcohol while you're pregnant, limit the amount that you drink. The Department of Health and Royal College of Obstetricians and Gynaecologists advise that pregnant women should not drink more than one to two units of alcohol once or twice a week. Binge drinking (drinking several units of alcohol in one session) should be avoided.

Caffeine

It is wise to limit the amount of caffeine you drink each day as it affects the way your body absorbs iron, which is very important for your baby's development. High levels of caffeine can result in a baby having a low birth weight or even miscarriage. Caffeine occurs naturally in coffee, tea and chocolate but is also added to some soft drinks and energy drinks. Some cold and flu remedies also contain caffeine, so always check with your pharmacist before taking any medicines while you're pregnant. It's important not to have more than 200mg of caffeine a day, which is roughly equivalent to:
* two mugs of instant coffee,
* one mug of filter coffee,
* two mugs of tea,
* five cans of regular cola, or
* four (50g) bars of plain chocolate

Fish to limit

Mackerel
Sardines
Trout
Tuna, fresh (tinned
    doesn't count as
    oily fish)

Fish to avoid

Marlin
Shark
Swordfish

Fish

When you're pregnant, don't eat too much of some types of fish. Oily fish is good for your health. However, you should limit how much you eat because it contains pollutants, such

as dioxins and PCBs (polychlorinated biphenyls). Pregnant women should eat no more than two portions of oily fish a week.

Don't eat fish that contains a high level of mercury as it can damage your baby's developing nervous system. Tuna contains a high level so don't eat more than two fresh tuna steaks or four medium-sized cans (about 140g per can) of tuna a week. This is about six rounds of tuna sandwiches or three tuna salads.

Also don't eat raw shellfish. This will reduce your chances of getting food poisoning, which can be particularly unpleasant when you're pregnant.

Campylobacter and salmonella

Campylobacter and salmonella are bacteria that can cause food poisoning. Campylobacter is found in raw meat and poultry, unpasteurised milk and untreated water and can cause miscarriage and early (premature) labour. Salmonella is found in raw meat and poultry, unpasteurised milk and raw eggs and raw egg products. Although salmonella food poisoning is unlikely to harm your baby, it's advisable to not eat foods that may contain salmonella.

To reduce your risk of getting campylobacter or salmonella food poisoning:

★ Don't eat foods containing raw or partially cooked eggs, such as homemade mayonnaise, and some mousses and sauces. Only eat eggs if they're cooked until both the white and the yolk are solid.
★ Don't eat unpasteurised dairy products.
★ Don't drink from a contaminated water supply.
★ Cook all meat and poultry thoroughly. Take extra care with products made from minced meat, such as sausages and burgers. Make sure they're cooked until piping hot all the way through and no pink meat is left.
★ Take extra care with meat at barbeques, parties and buffets. Bacteria breed quickly on food that's left uncovered in a warm place.

★ Make sure that raw meat doesn't come into contact with other food (e.g. in the fridge), particularly food that's already cooked, or food that will be eaten raw.
★ Always remember to wash your hands after handling or touching raw meat, or if you come into contact with animals.

Listeria

Listeriosis is a flu-like illness which you can get from food that contains listeria bacteria. Although it's rare in the UK, listeriosis can cause stillbirth, miscarriage or severe illness in newborn babies.

Don't eat foods where high levels of listeria are occasionally found:

★ Soft and blue-veined cheeses, such as camembert, brie and stilton. There's no risk of listeria from hard cheese such as cheddar or from cottage cheese or processed cheese.
★ Pâté: all types of pâté, including vegetable pâté.
★ Some prepared salads, such as potato salad and coleslaw.
★ Ready meals or reheated food, unless they're piping hot all the way through.

Toxoplasmosis

Toxoplasmosis is an infection caused by a parasite found in cat faeces. It can also be present in raw or undercooked meat, and soil left on unwashed fruit and vegetables. Although rare, toxoplasmosis can be passed to the unborn baby, which can cause serious problems.

To reduce the risk of toxoplasmosis, don't eat the following foods:

★ Unwashed raw fruit and vegetables,
★ Raw or undercooked meat,
★ Cured meats, such as Parma ham and salami
★ Unpasteurised goats' milk or goats' cheese.

You should also avoid contact with soil or faeces that might contain the toxoplasmosis parasite. Always wear gloves if you're gardening or changing a cat litter tray. If possible, ask someone else to do it for you.

useful resources

It is important when using pregnancy websites and parenting forums to look for a range of information from different websites as advice given from a personal standpoint may be biased and not entirely accurate.

EQUIP only links to websites that have been checked for the quality of their information (with links to resources in almost 100 languages). You can also search the directory of over 4000 national and local support groups and services which are checked regularly. This website has been created with the involvement of medical staff and members of the public.
www.equip.nhs.uk

The National Childbirth Trust is the UK's leading charity for parents. They help over a million mums and dads each year through pregnancy, birth and the early days of parenthood.
www.nct.org.uk

Direct.gov is a useful site – it is the one place where you will find all government advice and resources regarding pregnancy (e.g. information on maternity and paternity leave). For disabled parents, you can visit the Direct.gov section for all aspects of disability, pregnancy and parenthood among disabled parents.
www.direct.gov.uk/en/Parents/HavingABaby/HealthIn-Pregnancy/index.htm

Take a look at NHS Choices – the comprehensive National Health Service website, with antenatal information and an interactive pregnancy care planner.
www.nhs.uk

Wellbeing of Women – has a special offshoot website providing information on healthy eating and food safety both before and during pregnancy.
www.eatingforpregnancy.co.uk

Useful food and nutrition information
- Food Standards Agency – www.food.gov.uk and www.eatwell.gov.uk
- The British Dietetic Association – www.bda.uk.com
- The British Nutrition Foundation – www.nutrition.org.uk
- The Vegetarian Society – www.vegsoc.org
- The Vegan Society – www.vegansociety.com
- Diabetes UK – www.diabetes.org.uk

vegetarian and vegan tips

Vegetarianism can be an extremely healthy lifestyle for pregnant women, especially because studies show that vegetarians are more likely to consume whole grains, legumes and vegetables than meat eaters and daily dietary requirements tend to be very easy to come by. Vegans, however, need to be diligent about making sure that during pregnancy they get all the important nutrients usually associated with meat and dairy – especially protein, iron, calcium, vitamins D and B12, zinc and folate.

Good vegan protein sources

Soya products (soya milk, tofu, tempeh)
Beans and other legumes
Nuts/nut butters
Whole grains (especially quinoa)

Vitamin D aids in the absorption of calcium, but few foods naturally contain it. Still, it is easily found in fortified milk products and ready-to-eat cereals. For vegans, fortified soya milk is a good source, but it's still worth asking your health-care provider if you should take a supplement.

Out of all the B vitamins, B12 is the biggest concern for vegetarians and vegans as it is found mainly in animal products. Pregnant women who avoid meat need to make a concerted effort to eat plant-based food sources of vitamin B12, such as fortified soya milk, to prevent anaemia. A fortified breakfast cereal with milk or fortified soya milk is a great and healthy way to get your B12.

Useful resources, Australia
- Pregnancy Help Australia – a national body which provides support, education and resources to Pregnancy Support Centres throughout Australia.
www.pregnancysupport.com.au
- The National Health and Medical Research Council – www.nhmrc.gov.au
- Women's Health Statewide – www.whs.sa.gov.au
- The Dietitians Association Australia – www.daa.asn.au
- Australian vegetarian society – www.veg-soc.org
- The Vegan Society – www.vegansociety.com
- Diabetes Australia – www.diabetesaustralia.com.au

good go-to snacks

During pregnancy, eating enough to keep your blood sugar stable as well as meeting the nutritional needs of you and your growing baby is often a challenge. Go too long and your body will certainly let you know; as you can probably attest, there is no desperation like that of a hungry pregnant woman. That's why it's a good idea to keep snacks on hand at all times. Stick a few in your bag or lunch box and you'll be able to tame your tummy before it starts to roar.

1   Low-fat yogurt
2   Apple with nut butter
3   Peanut Butter Chocolate Chip Energy Bars*
4   Sesame-Honey Almonds*
5   Cheese strings
6   Hummus and Crudités*
7   Fruit Salad with Orange-Ginger Syrup*
8   Fortified ready-to-eat cereal
9   Glass of skimmed milk or soya milk
10 Edamame or roasted soya beans

* See recipes

sleep

The art of sleep becomes a whole new skill when you are pregnant. The fact is, your body is going through a multitude of changes in its growth and hormones, and these tend to disrupt sleep. A change of sleeping position may bring relief. Try lying on your side, with your lower leg bent at the knee to support your tummy. Sleeping with a pillow between your legs may also help. Ironically, getting enough sleep is important for you and your baby.

Here are some things you can try to improve slumber.

1   Avoid drinking too much for an hour before bed, but be sure to stay well hydrated during the day.

2   To prevent heartburn from keeping you awake, don't lie flat on your back for 1–2 hours after eating.

3   Exercise may help you sleep better by improving your circulation and easing stress.

4   Turn off all electronics well before bedtime, and allow yourself to fully shut off. Simple relaxation techniques can help you get to sleep. Concentrate on breathing gently and rhythmically, and contract and relax each part of your body one at a time.

5   Try drinking Warm Vanilla Milk (page 138) or have a cup of herbal tea.

exercise

If you don't have a high-risk pregnancy, exercise is extremely beneficial to both you and your baby. Proper exercise can help keep your weight gain under control and can lessen common pregnancy complaints such as sore legs and stiffness. Exercise can also boost your energy level and may even shorten labour and recovery time. But it's important to remember that pregnancy is not the time to try to lose weight or achieve any major fitness goal like running a marathon.

However, exercising even just three to four days per week for at least 20–30 minutes will have tremendous health benefits for you and your baby. Here are some important exercise guidelines to to keep you and your baby safe and healthy.

1   Do both aerobic (which gets your heart working harder) and strength-conditioning (that is designed to make your muscles stronger) exercise while pregnant.

2   Do not exercise lying on your back and avoid sports or exercise that increases the chance of trauma, e.g. skiing, horse riding and contact sports like kickboxing, scuba diving.

3   Make sure that you are well hydrated and don't allow yourself to get overheated or exercise in hot humid conditions.

4   Don't allow yourself to get overheated.

5   Resume your workouts gradually after giving birth and only when your healthcare provider gives you the go-ahead.

let's get cooking

Now that you know what your body needs and why, here's the fun part: you can easily nourish yourself and your baby by whipping up the outstanding dishes in the following pages! Because there is no 'perfect' diet for the pregnant woman, all you need to do is to cook and savour a wide variety of the recipes. Even better is that each one was created with the busy mum-to-be in mind, which means they are made from readily available ingredients and easy and quick to prepare.

Now, I know you've got the appetite, so please bite into the following recipes unabashedly! If you're like me, you will find that they are tasty and practical enough to return to once you have a larger family to feed, especially because many of them are kid-friendly and so easy to prepare that you can practically whip them up with a baby hanging off your hip!

storecupboard essentials

Make life easy on yourself and stock up on storecupboard essentials that you will regularly reach for when cooking from this book:

- olive oil
- rapeseed oil
- red wine vinegar
- white wine vinegar
- sherry wine vinegar
- cartons of chicken or vegetable stock
- soy sauce
- old-fashioned rolled (porridge) oats
- flaked almonds
- maple syrup
- honey
- vanilla
- sea salt
- black peppercorns
- Dijon mustard
- garlic
- fresh ginger

It wouldn't hurt to add some berries and carrots, eggs, fat-free Greek yogurt and frozen prawns to your shopping basket, since they are great last-minute go-to ingredients or easily prepared mini meals, even if you're not cooking from this book.

chapter one

breakfast

nutrient-rich granola

The great thing about granola is that it's easy to make in bulk and even easier to customise. Plus, it can serve as a wholesome, energy-rich breakfast or snack when paired with milk or sprinkled over yogurt or cottage cheese. This particular mixture maximises the health factor with omega-3-rich pumpkin seeds and protein-packed peanuts and oats, which are full of dietary fibre. Feel free to add other nuts, dried fruit or both!

Serves 16

240g rolled (porridge) oats
65g pumpkin seeds
55g flaked almonds
50g soft dark brown sugar
3 tablespoons runny honey

4 tablespoons vegetable oil
1½ teaspoons ground cardamom
½ teaspoon sea salt
80g raisins

Preheat the oven to 120°C/250°F/Gas Mark ½.

Combine the oats, pumpkin seeds, flaked almonds and brown sugar in a large bowl.

In a separate bowl, combine the honey, oil, cardamom and salt. Mix both bowls together and spread the mixture evenly on 1 large or 2 smaller baking trays. Bake for 1¼ hours, stirring every 15 minutes for an even colour.

Remove from the oven, leave to cool and transfer to a large bowl. Add the raisins and mix until evenly distributed.

PER SERVING: 176 CALORIES, 8.62G FAT, 1.09G CARBS, 5.28G PROTEIN, 2.33G FIBRE, 23MG CALCIUM, 2.03MG IRON, 75MG SODIUM, 10μG FOLATE

yogurt, granola and strawberry parfait

An ideal way to start a morning or satisfy midday hunger pangs, this fruit, yogurt and granola combo looks beautiful when layered in a dessert glass but tastes just as good if served in a bowl. And it provides protein, dietary fibre, vitamin C, folate and potassium.

Serves 1

185g Greek yogurt
1 teaspoon runny honey
30g granola (shop-bought or see recipe on this page)
100g fresh organic strawberries, hulled and quartered
fresh mint sprig, to decorate (optional)

Place the yogurt in a glass or bowl. Drizzle with the honey, top with the granola, and finish with a layer of strawberries.

Decorate with a mint sprig, if you like. Bon appétit!

PER SERVING: 311 CALORIES, 7.53G FAT, 45.73G CARBS, 15.91G PROTEIN, FIBRE, 407MG CALCIUM, 2.00MG IRON, 149MG SODIUM, 76μG FOLATE

maple porridge with raisins and almonds

Wonderfully filling and containing heart-healthy fibre and antioxidants, oatmeal is also an excellent source of manganese, a mineral that helps you and your baby form bone and cartilage.

Serves 1

125ml water
125ml semi-skimmed milk
¼ teaspoon sea salt
40g rolled (porridge) oats
½ teaspoon vanilla extract
1 tablespoon raisins
2 teaspoons toasted flaked almonds
1 tablespoon pure maple syrup

Bring the water, milk and salt to the boil in a small saucepan. Add the oats and vanilla extract, reduce the heat to low and cook for 10–20 minutes, stirring occasionally, until it is the desired consistency. Add additional water if necessary.

Transfer the porridge to a serving bowl and top with the raisins and almonds. Drizzle with the maple syrup.

PER SERVING: 328 CALORIES, 5.39G FAT, 59.67G CARBS, 11.56G PROTEIN, 4.75G FIBRE, 225MG CALCIUM, 2.58MG IRON, 659MG SODIUM, 20µG FOLATE

asparagus, gruyère and shallot scramble

The dynamic combo of rich cheese, sweet caramelised shallots and fresh asparagus should be enough reason to break out your frying pan and whip up this quick breakfast, which is my mum's recipe. But here's an even better excuse: asparagus imparts excellent amounts of folate (which is essential for a baby's development, especially during early pregnancy), and eggs and cheese are wonderful protein sources.

Serves 4

2 teaspoons rapeseed oil
10g unsalted butter
70g finely chopped shallots
20 asparagus spears (green parts only), sliced at
  an angle into 6mm pieces
8 medium eggs
4 teaspoons water
½ teaspoon sea salt
pinch of freshly ground black pepper
175g Gruyère cheese, grated

Heat the oil and butter in a large, non-stick frying pan over a medium heat. Add the shallots and asparagus and cook until the asparagus is cooked but still has a slight crunch and the shallots have not yet browned.

Mix together the eggs, water and salt and pepper in a bowl, then add to the pan. Sprinkle the grated cheese on top of the egg mixture and gently stir until the eggs are fully cooked. Serve hot.

PER SERVING: 294 CALORIES, 18.42G FAT, 5.65G CARBS, 22.66G PROTEIN, 1.68G FIBRE, 348 MG CALCIUM, 3.71MG IRON, 233MG SODIUM, 94µG FOLATE

portobello and black bean breakfast burritos

Robustly flavoured by meaty portobello mushrooms, this vegetarian meal can be prepared in advance. Refrigerate or freeze a couple of burritos for a quick protein-rich meal later.

Serves 4

4 large flour tortillas
1 tablespoon plus 1 teaspoon olive oil
1 small onion, diced
1 tablespoon finely chopped garlic
2 large portobello mushrooms, diced
3 tablespoons freshly squeezed lemon juice
1 tablespoon brown rice miso paste
1 tablespoon hoisin sauce
½ teaspoon sea salt
dash of Tabasco sauce, or to taste
260g canned black beans, rinsed and drained
195g cooked brown rice
4 medium egg whites
60g Cheddar cheese, grated (optional)
110g salsa (optional)

Preheat the oven to 180°C/350°F/Gas Mark 4. Wrap the tortillas tightly in a large sheet of foil and warm in the oven for 10–15 minutes until heated through. Keep warm.

Meanwhile, heat the oil in a large frying pan until hot but not smoking. Cook the onion, garlic and mushrooms for 8–10 minutes, stirring occasionally, until browned.

Whisk together the lemon juice, miso paste, hoisin sauce, salt and Tabasco in a small bowl. Pour over the mushrooms, transfer to a food processor and pulse until well chopped but not pulverised. Return to the pan and add the black beans, brown rice and egg whites. Cook over a medium heat, stirring, until the egg whites are fully cooked.

Place a warm tortilla on a plate. Spoon a quarter of the mushroom mixture, a quarter of the cheese and a quarter of the salsa, if using, in vertical rows across the centre, leaving room on the bottom and sides of the tortilla. Fold the bottom over most of the filling, then fold over the sides so that they overlap. Repeat with the other 3 burritos. Serve hot.

PER SERVING: 642 CALORIES, 12.52G FAT, 84.48G CARBS, 7.50G FIBRE, 21.60G PROTEIN, 255MG CALCIUM, 4.10MG IRON, 1125MG SODIUM, 101µG FOLATE

courgettes, basil and parmesan frittata

This vegetarian dish is a basil, courgette and red pepper riff on famed New York chef Eric Ripert's Zucchini [Courgette] Mint Parmesan Frittata. It does double duty as a healthy way to start the day or a perfect lunch partner, especially if paired with a small green salad.

Serves 6

8 large eggs
2 courgettes, thinly sliced
1 roasted red pepper, deseeded and julienned
25g Parmesan cheese, freshly grated
20 basil leaves, torn into pieces
½ teaspoon sea salt
freshly ground black pepper
1–1½ teaspoons olive oil

Preheat the oven to 160°C/325°F/Gas Mark 3.

Whisk the eggs well in a bowl. Add the courgettes, roasted red pepper, Parmesan and basil, season to taste and stir to combine.

Heat the oil in a 23–25cm ovenproof frying pan over a medium heat, swirling the oil to coat the base and side. Pour in the egg mixture and cook, without stirring, for 3 minutes, or until it begins to pull away from the pan.

Transfer the pan to the oven and bake for 12–15 minutes, or until the eggs are set and firm in the centre.

Gently run a rubber spatula around the side of the pan to loosen the frittata. For an elegant presentation, place a serving plate over the pan and carefully flip the pan to invert the frittata onto the plate. Cut into wedges or simply serve straight from the pan.

PER SERVING: 164 CALORIES, 8.05G FAT, 6.14G CARBS, 13.23G PROTEIN, 2.42G FIBRE, 232MG CALCIUM, 4.11MG IRON, 163MG SODIUM, 113µG FOLATE

cottage cheese and strawberry pancake 'omelettes'

A denser, more nutritious answer to a breakfast favourite, these extra-moist pancakes are served folded like an omelette, stuffed with sliced strawberries, drizzled with maple syrup and sprinkled with icing sugar – all of which makes them look and taste like dessert. Be sure to use organic strawberries, which include all the fruit's nutrients without the pesticides found in non-organic options. You will also increase the health factor if you opt for wholemeal flour.

Serves 4

150g low-fat cottage cheese
140g wholemeal flour
2 large eggs
4 medium egg whites
2 tablespoons runny honey
2 tablespoons semi-skimmed milk
1 teaspoon vanilla extract
¼ teaspoon ground cinnamon
pinch of sea salt
1 teaspoon rapeseed oil
280g fresh organic strawberries,
    hulled and sliced
4 teaspoons maple syrup
2 teaspoons icing sugar
4 fresh mint sprigs, to garnish (optional)

Preheat the oven to 110°C/225°F/Gas Mark ¼. In a large bowl, mix together the cottage cheese, flour, eggs, egg whites, honey, milk, vanilla extract, cinnamon and salt.

Heat the oil in a large non-stick frying pan over a medium heat, swirling the oil to coat the base of the pan. Pour a quarter of the batter into the pan, tilting so that it spreads evenly and thinly. Cook for about 3 minutes until the bottom is brown and bubbles form on top. Flip and cook for a further 3 minutes, or until brown on the other side and the pancake is cooked through. Transfer to a plate and keep warm in the oven. Repeat with the remaining batter until there are 4 pancakes.

When all the pancakes are cooked, transfer each to a plate, top with a quarter of the sliced strawberries and drizzle with 1 teaspoon of maple syrup. Fold the pancake in half so that it is shaped like an omelette. Sprinkle with the icing sugar and garnish with a mint sprig, if you like. Repeat with the remaining 'omelettes' and serve.

PER SERVING: 282 CALORIES, 4.41G FAT, 45.16G CARBS, 5.52G FIBRE, 16.25G PROTEIN, 92MG CALCIUM, 2.37MG IRON, 294MG SODIUM, 51μG FOLATE

totally tasty
breakfast muffins

Taking the lead from James Peterson, author of award-winning book *Baking*, this recipe makes impossibly moist, dessert-like muffins. They are loaded with vegetables, good fats (from the nuts and seeds) – which are essential for a developing baby brain – and even fresh fruit. Snack on them for a week or freeze a batch for future late-night snack attacks. They're a great way to get vegetables, fibre and antioxidants without even working for it!

Makes 12 muffins

butter, for greasing (optional)
90g plain flour, plus extra for flouring the tin (optional)
65g caster sugar
1 teaspoon bicarbonate of soda
¾ teaspoon baking powder
1 teaspoon ground cinnamon
¼ teaspoon freshly grated nutmeg
¼ teaspoon ground allspice
¼ teaspoon sea salt
75ml vegetable oil
2 medium eggs
45g pumpkin seeds (optional)
115g shelled walnuts, chopped
75g finely grated courgettes
70g peeled, cored and finely grated sweet red apple
90g peeled carrot, finely grated

Preheat the oven to 180°C/350°F/Gas Mark 4. Grease and flour the muffin tin if it isn't non-stick.

Sift together the flour, sugar, bicarbonate of soda, baking powder, cinnamon, nutmeg, allspice and salt into a bowl, and mix to combine.

Whisk together the oil and eggs in a small bowl until blended, then stir into the flour mixture.

In a coffee grinder or food processor, grind the pumpkin seeds into a coarse flour. Mix into the muffin mixture with the walnuts, courgettes, apple and carrot.

Divide the muffin mixture evenly between the 12 muffin cups and bake for 15–18 minutes, or until a cocktail stick inserted in the centre comes out clean. Leave to cool on a wire rack, then run a knife around the edge of each muffin and gently remove from the tin.

PER SERVING: 220 CALORIES, 15.93G FAT, 15.09G CARBS, 1.59G FIBRE, 5.36G PROTEIN, 41MG CALCIUM, 1.82MG IRON, 202MG SODIUM, 31µG FOLATE

ricotta cheese blintzes with blueberry sauce

Let's be honest: these dessert-like breakfast treats are not exactly pillars of healthy eating. However, of all the sweet, syrup-laden day-starters out there, these do a good job of providing protein from the ricotta and vitamin C, dietary fibre and antioxidants from the blueberries, as well as all-around satisfaction. They also look pretty enough to be special-occasion fare. Want to make them more guilt free? Use the ripest, sweetest blueberries you can find and cut back on the amount of sugar you use. Or skip the blueberries altogether and top with sliced strawberries.

Serves 4

2 medium eggs
4 tablespoons skimmed milk
75ml water
1 tablespoon vegetable oil
90g plain flour
¼ teaspoon plus 2 tablespoons caster sugar
pinch of sea salt
butter or cooking spray, for greasing
245g ricotta cheese
40g icing sugar
finely grated zest of ½ unwaxed lemon
2 tablespoons freshly squeezed lemon juice
150g fresh organic blueberries
¾ teaspoon cornflour

In a large bowl, beat together 1 egg with the milk, water and oil. Beat in the flour, the ¼ teaspoon of caster sugar and the salt until smooth.

Heat a medium non-stick frying pan over a medium-high heat. Ladle a quarter of the batter into the pan, tilting so that it evenly coats the base. Cook for 2–4 minutes until light brown on both sides, turning once. Transfer to a platter and repeat with the remaining batter, separating the crêpes with small squares of greaseproof paper.

Preheat the oven to 180°C/350°F/Gas Mark 4. Grease a 23cm x 33cm baking dish with butter or spray with cooking oil.

Beat the remaining egg in a bowl and stir in the ricotta, icing sugar, lemon zest and 1 tablespoon of lemon juice. Spoon about 2 tablespoons of this mixture onto a crêpe, then fold up the top and bottom like an envelope, tucking the ends in to keep the filling from spilling out. Repeat with the remaining ingredients until there are 4 blintzes. Arrange in the baking dish and bake for 20 minutes.

Combine the blueberries, the remaining 1 tablespoon of lemon juice, the 2 tablespoons of caster sugar and the cornflour in a saucepan and cook over a medium heat, stirring frequently, for about 5 minutes until the berries burst. Remove from the heat and keep warm.

To serve, place 1 blintz on a plate and top with a quarter of the berry mixture.

PER SERVING: 346 CALORIES, 13.37G FAT, 43.10G CARBS, 2.12G FIBRE, 13.21G PROTEIN, 185MG CALCIUM, 1.15MG IRON, 168MG SODIUM, 27µG FOLATE

chapter two
snacks

roasted carrot chews

When easy-to-grab snacks are essential to everyday sanity, it's a good idea to have healthy options on hand. These rustic, chewy, sweet and salty carrot bites rise to the appetite-curbing occasion, and they taste great too. Even better, carrots are brimming with good stuff, including vitamins A, C, K and B6, potassium and fibre. Want to jazz them up? Sprinkle them with a tablespoon of finely chopped parsley leaves.

Serves 4

10 large carrots, peeled
2 teaspoons olive oil
1 teaspoon sea salt, plus extra to taste

Preheat the oven to 200°C/400°F/Gas Mark 6.

Slice the carrots lengthwise into long batons. Toss them in a bowl with the oil and salt until they are evenly coated. Spread the carrots on a baking tray in a single layer and roast for 30 minutes.

Leave the carrots to cool, season with additional salt, if you like, and snack in good conscience.

PER SERVING: 93 CALORIES, 2.49G FAT, 17.24G CARBS, 1.67G PROTEIN, 5.04G FIBRE, 59 MG CALCIUM, 0.56MG IRON, 705MG SODIUM, 34µG FOLATE

parmesan-dusted kale crisps

No need to force yourself to eat dark leafy greens with this genius recipe from *The Real Deal Guide to Pregnancy*'s website, realdealguide.com. The crunchy texture and delicious flavour of these 'crisps' garner almost the same adoration as the less-nutritional potato-based bites but unlike their greasier competition, they're super-low in calories and loaded with vitamins A, C and K – not to mention that kale is a better source of calcium than spinach!

Serves 4

1 bunch of curly kale
1 tablespoon olive oil
25g Parmesan cheese, freshly grated

Preheat the oven to 120°C/250°F/Gas Mark ½.

Cut out the central stems of the kale leaves and discard. Slice each kale leaf into 10cm pieces, toss them in a bowl with the oil, then evenly sprinkle with the Parmesan.

Spread the kale on a baking sheet in a single layer and bake for 30 minutes, or until crisp.

Serve warm and unabashedly.

PER SERVING: 90 CALORIES, 5.28G FAT, 6.96G CARBS, 4.61G PROTEIN, 1.34G FIBRE, 159MG CALCIUM, 1.21MG IRON, 124MG SODIUM, 19µG FOLATE

peanut butter chocolate chip energy bars

You can't beat snacks that are freshly made with wholesome ingredients. Modestly sweet with a flavour boost of salt, these peanut butter bites are chock-full of protein and folate, both of which are extremely important during pregnancy.

Makes 20 bars

vegetable oil, for oiling
80g quick-cooking rolled (porridge) oats
150g dry-roasted peanuts
130g peanut butter
65g sunflower seeds
20 Medjool dates, stoned
2 medium eggs
1 teaspoon sea salt
1 teaspoon vanilla extract
90g dark chocolate chips

Preheat the oven to 180°C/350°F/Gas Mark 4. Lightly oil a 23cm square baking tin and line the base with baking parchment.

Put the oats, peanuts, peanut butter, sunflower seeds and dates in a food processor and pulse until finely chopped.

Whisk the eggs together with the salt and vanilla extract, then add to the food processor and pulse until the mixture becomes a coarse, chunky paste. Mix in the chocolate chips by hand. Transfer the mixture to the prepared baking tin and spread evenly, gently pressing down to flatten. Bake for 35 minutes, or until firm and golden.

Cool and cut into 20 bars. Store in an airtight container for a week in the fridge and a month in the freezer.

PER BAR: 164 CALORIES, 10.31G FAT, 14.51G CARBS, 5.39G PROTEIN, 2.57G FIBRE, 16MG CALCIUM, 1.00MG IRON, 153MG SODIUM, 28µG FOLATE

sesame-honey almonds

A fantastic on-the-go snack and treat all in one, these protein- and calcium-loaded almonds are best made in bulk so that you can grab a handful whenever you want. The only challenge is not to eat them all in a single sitting.

Serves 16

430g sesame seeds
½ teaspoon coarse sea salt
5 tablespoons runny honey
2 tablespoons granulated sugar
435g whole blanched almonds

Preheat the oven to 180°C/350°F/Gas Mark 4.

Place the sesame seeds in a large bowl and sprinkle the salt evenly over them.

Heat the honey and sugar in a saucepan over a medium heat, stirring until the mixture is runny. Working in batches, add the almonds to the hot mixture and stir to coat. Quickly remove with a slotted spoon, letting the extra liquid drain off, and transfer the nuts to the bowl of sesame seeds.

Stir the nuts to coat with the sesame seeds, then transfer to a baking parchment-lined baking tray.

Repeat until all the nuts are coated. Bake the sesame-coated almonds for 10–12 minutes.

Cool completely and store in an airtight container with a tight-sealing lid.

PER SERVING: 316 CALORIES, 23.49G FAT, 18.94G CARBS, 9.77G PROTEIN, 6.63G FIBRE, 307MG CALCIUM, 4.56MG IRON, 75M SODIUM, 36µG FOLATE

japanese-style cold tofu

If you need a quick protein fix and your palate is craving pure, clean flavours, try this traditional Japanese dish. Called *hiyayakko*, it's elegant, easy to prepare and refreshingly cold – making it perfect for cooling the engine and appetite of the overheated mother-to-be. Don't worry if you can't find bonito flakes. While they add interesting texture and a hint of fish flavour, the dish also works without them.

Serves 4

4 x 80g pieces of silken tofu
4 teaspoons chopped spring onion
1 teaspoon peeled and grated fresh ginger
8 teaspoons dried bonito flakes (*katsuobushi*)
4 teaspoons low-sodium soy sauce

Place the tofu in 4 individual bowls. Top each piece with 1 teaspoon of spring onion, ¼ teaspoon of grated ginger and 2 teaspoons of bonito flakes.

Pour 1 teaspoon of soy sauce over each piece of tofu and enjoy!

PER SERVING: 64 CALORIES, 1.96G FAT, 2.57G CARBS, 6.21G PROTEIN, 0.21G FIBRE, 28MG CALCIUM, 1.02MG IRON, 364MG SODIUM, 2µG FOLATE

cucumber and mint sandwiches

Sometimes the simplest pleasures are the best, and this little sandwich proves the point. As easy to make as it is to love, it combines the clean, refreshing flavours of cucumber and mint with salted butter and wholemeal bread. Since mint can help settle a fussy stomach, these bites are also great for morning sickness. Enjoy with a cup of nice rooibos tea with a dash of milk.

Serves 4

25g salted butter, softened
4 tablespoons finely chopped fresh mint, plus extra leaves to garnish (optional)
coarsely ground black pepper
2 slices of wholemeal bread, crusts trimmed if you like
¼ cucumber, peeled and sliced into thin rounds

Mix together the butter, mint and pepper to taste. Spread each slice of bread thinly with mint butter and top with layers of cucumber.

Slice the open sandwiches in half, garnish with mint leaves, if you like, and serve.

PER SERVING: 90 CALORIES, 5.79G FAT, 7.33G CARBS, 1.77G PROTEIN, 0.96G FIBRE, 34MG CALCIUM, 1.18MG IRON, 107MG SODIUM, 18µG FOLATE

hummus and crudités

One sure-fire way to avoid reaching for food that's bad for you the minute you feel hungry is to keep this snack on hand at all times. Easily stored in the fridge, hummus with healthy things to dip in it can be a life-saver for the famished mum-to-be – and a good source of dietary fibre, protein and folate.

Serves 8

1 tablespoon crushed garlic
½ teaspoon sea salt
450g tinned chickpeas, rinsed and drained
125g well-stirred tahini (sesame seed paste)
3 tablespoons freshly squeezed lemon juice
½ teaspoon white wine vinegar
2 tablespoons olive oil
¼ teaspoon ground cumin
2 tablespoons water
4 carrots, peeled and cut into batons
1 cucumber, peeled and cut into batons
2 red peppers, deseeded and cut into batons

Put the garlic, salt, chickpeas, tahini, lemon juice, vinegar, oil, cumin and water in a food processor and blend until smooth. Transfer to a small serving dish.

Serve the hummus with the carrot, cucumber and red pepper batons.

PER SERVING: 176 CALORIES, 7.73G FAT, 22.05G CARBS, 5.21G PROTEIN, 4.92G FIBRE, 51MG CALCIUM, 1.54MG IRON, 354MG SODIUM, 73µG FOLATE

crudités with lemon-dill dip

Most creamy dips use calorie-heavy mayonnaise or soured cream as a base. But this one leverages the tangy deliciousness of Greek yogurt, making it guilt-free as well as nutritious. While you could easily devour all four servings in one sitting without concern, you can also store it in an airtight container in the fridge for up to three days.

Serves 4

245g fat-free Greek yogurt
2 tablespoons finely chopped fresh dill, plus extra
    to garnish (optional)
1 teaspoon freshly squeezed lemon juice
¼ teaspoon coarse sea salt
freshly ground black pepper
4 celery sticks, sliced into batons
1 cucumber, peeled and sliced into batons
2 large carrots, peeled and sliced into batons
lemon wedge, to serve (optional)

Mix together the yogurt, dill and lemon juice in a small bowl and season to taste. Transfer to a small serving bowl.

Serve the dip with the celery, cucumber and carrot batons, garnished with extra dill and with a lemon wedge for squeezing over, if you like.

PER SERVING: 63 CALORIES, 0.24G FAT, 10.98G CARBS, 4.55G PROTEIN, 2.15G FIBRE, 159MG CALCIUM, 0.42MG IRON, 250MG SODIUM, 38µG FOLATE

broad bean, tomato, avocado and corn salsa

This dish is easy to prepare and perfect as a snack with toasted pitta. It's also flexible enough that you can substitute whatever vegetables you like best (think courgettes, peppers and even lightly steamed broccoli or green beans). Best of all, it's really healthy.

Serves 4

675g fresh broad beans
150g cherry tomatoes
½ firm, ripe avocado, stoned, peeled and diced
1 corn on the cob (cooked or raw)
2 tablespoons extra virgin olive oil
2 teaspoons sherry vinegar
1 tablespoon diced shallot or red onion
1 teaspoon granulated sugar
½ teaspoon sea salt, or to taste
freshly ground black pepper

Cook the broad beans in a large saucepan of boiling water for 4 minutes. Drain, cool in a bowl of iced water and then pierce and peel away the skins. Place the peeled beans in a serving bowl.

Halve the tomatoes and add them to the bowl. Gently add the avocado so that it keeps its shape. Cut the corn kernels off the cob and add to the bowl.

In a small bowl, whisk together the oil, vinegar, shallot, and sugar and season to taste.

Gently toss the salad with the dressing, add additional seasoning if necessary and serve immediately.

PER SERVING: 280 CALORIES, 11.28G FAT, 39.35G CARBS, 15.09G PROTEIN, 2.74G FIBRE, 70MG CALCIUM, 3.07MG IRON, 340MG SODIUM, 288µG FOLATE

fruit salad with orange-ginger syrup

Nausea-soothing ginger adds extra oomph to this classic, simple snack. Don't hesitate to substitute your favourite fruit or serve this over natural yogurt. Everything tastes better when coated in sweet ginger syrup!

Serves 4

2 tablespoons freshly squeezed orange juice
1 tablespoon peeled and finely chopped fresh ginger
2 tablespoons runny honey
½ medium cantaloupe melon, peeled, deseeded and
   cut into bite-sized chunks
280g fresh organic strawberries, hulled and sliced
145g fresh organic blueberries
1 crisp red apple, cored and cut into bite-sized pieces
150g seedless grapes
4 fresh mint leaves, sliced into extra-thin strips

Warm the orange juice with the ginger in a small saucepan over a medium heat for about 4 minutes, or just until it begins to simmer.

Strain and discard the ginger, reserving the juice in a serving bowl. Mix in the honey until well combined. Add the fruit and mint and toss thoroughly to coat. Cover and chill for at least 30 minutes or up to 4 hours.

PER SERVING: 162 CALORIES, 0.52G FAT, 41.50G CARBS, 2.10G PROTEIN, 5.03G FIBRE, 34MG CALCIUM, 1.19MG IRON, 13MG SODIUM, 43µG FOLATE

artichokes with tarragon dip

Artichokes are a fabulous source of fibre and vitamin C, and Greek yogurt adds a shot of protein to the lemony, tarragon-tinged accompaniment. Serve these warm or cold – they're great either way.

Serves 4

1 lemon, halved
4 tablespoons low-fat mayonnaise
4 tablespoons fat-free natural yogurt
4 teaspoons finely chopped fresh tarragon
2 teaspoons Dijon mustard
generous pinch of freshly ground black pepper
sea salt
4 globe artichokes

Squeeze the juice from 1 of the lemon halves, reserving the squeezed lemon half.

Combine the mayonnaise, yogurt, tarragon, mustard, black pepper and 2 teaspoons of the lemon juice in a small bowl. Transfer to a small serving bowl and refrigerate, covered, for at least 30 minutes.

Fill a large saucepan with salted water and bring to the boil. Trim the top and bottom of each artichoke. Place the artichokes and the squeezed lemon half in the boiling water, cover and cook at a brisk simmer for about 30–45 minutes, until a sharp knife goes through the base of each artichoke with ease.

Drain and serve with the tarragon dip.

PER SERVING: 125 CALORIES, 5.03G FAT, 19.22G CARBS, 5.77G PROTEIN, 8.33G FIBRE, 112MG CALCIUM, 2.14MG IRON, 262MG SODIUM, 90µG FOLATE

niçoise salad wheels

Fast to prepare, high in protein, niacin and vitamin B12 and easy to store for surprise hunger attacks, this tuna-cucumber temptation is a safe snack. Just be sure to limit your intake of skipjack or yellowfin tuna and other low-mercury fish to 350g per week. You can also swap the cucumber wheels for crackers.

Serves 4

4 teaspoons extra virgin olive oil
2 teaspoons red wine vinegar
freshly ground black pepper
8 Kalamata olives, stoned and finely chopped
2 tablespoons finely chopped red onion
1 x 185g tin skipjack or yellowfin tuna in spring water
1 cucumber, peeled and sliced into 16 x 1cm-thick wheels

Combine the oil, vinegar, pepper to taste, olives and onion in a non-reactive bowl. Cover and leave to stand for 15 minutes.

Drain the tuna, transfer to a small serving bowl and add the vinaigrette. Gently stir to combine.

Serve with cucumber wheels.

PER SERVING: 73 CALORIES, 5.29G FAT, 2.01G CARBS, 4.13G PROTEIN, 0.73G FIBRE, 14MG CALCIUM, 0.46MG IRON, 133MG SODIUM, 10µG FOLATE

margherita toast

not-so-naughty nachos

Have your pizza and eat it too with this single-serving taste of Italy. Easy to prepare and a better bet than a whole pizza for those seeking help with portion control, it can also be customised to your liking – just add sliced mushrooms, olives, chopped peppers, pineapple or anything else you like.

Serves 1

1 tablespoon bottled tomato pasta sauce
½ wholemeal English muffin or slice of bread, toasted
1 thin slice of reduced-fat mozzarella cheese
5 fresh basil leaves

Preheat the grill.

Spread the tomato sauce on the muffin half and top with the mozzarella and basil.

Grill for about 5 minutes, or until the cheese has melted.

PER SERVING: 163 CALORIES, 6.29G FAT, 16.68G CARBS, 10.54G PROTEIN, 2.67G FIBRE, 298MG CALCIUM, 1.07MG IRON, 367MG SODIUM, 21µG FOLATE

The key to success with this health-friendly version of classic nachos is to make sure you've got friends to help you polish off the plate. Just make a quarter of the recipe when snacking solo so that you don't overeat.

Serves 4

18 (about 25g) baked natural tortilla chips
60g Cheddar cheese, finely grated
1 heaped tablespoon deseeded and diced ripe tomato
20g firm avocado flesh, diced
1 tablespoon sliced spring onion
1 tablespoon sliced preserved jalapeño chillies, chopped
sea salt

Preheat the grill.

Scatter the tortilla chips on a baking tray covered with foil. Sprinkle the cheese on top of the chips and grill for about 3–4 minutes, or just until the cheese has melted.

Sprinkle the tomato, avocado, spring onion, jalapeño and a little salt over the nachos and serve.

PER SERVING: 102 CALORIES, 5.74G FAT, 7.80G CARBS, 4.74G PROTEIN, 1.26G FIBRE, 118MG CALCIUM, 0.39MG IRON, 154MG SODIUM, 14µG FOLATE

grilled cheese sandwich gone good

While nothing beats the classic butter-saturated sandwich fully loaded with melted Cheddar, Fontina or Gruyère, there is a healthier way to get your grease on. And this sandwich is it. Want to liven it up? Go ahead and add a slice of tomato, ham or both before cooking. You deserve it!

Serves 1

½ teaspoon extra-virgin olive oil
2 slices of wholemeal bread
1 thick slice of Cheddar or mozzarella cheese

Preheat the oven to 180°C/350°F/Gas Mark 4.

Heat the olive oil in a small ovenproof frying pan over a medium heat, tilting the pan so that the oil evenly coats the base, until it is hot but not smoking. Add a slice of bread, then layer with the cheese and the second slice of bread. Cook the sandwich for about 2 minutes until the underside is crisp and golden, then flip to toast the other side.

Transfer to the oven for 5–7 minutes, or until the cheese is melted. Enjoy!

PER SERVING: 264 CALORIES, 12.52G FAT, 24.11G CARBS, 12.43G PROTEIN, 1.80G FIBRE, 272MG CALCIUM, 1.93MG IRON, 433MG SODIUM, 47µG FOLATE

herbed parmesan popcorn

While popcorn isn't exactly the pinnacle of nutrition, it's a fantastically light snack when prepared without gobs of oil, or butter. Incidentally, you can change these toppings quite easily: just swap the Parmesan and parsley for curry powder, nutritional yeast or garlic powder.

Serves 1

1½ tablespoons popcorn kernels
olive oil spray
2 tablespoons freshly grated Parmesan cheese
¼ teaspoon sea salt
½ teaspoon dried parsley

Put the popcorn kernels in a large paper bag, then fold over the top a couple of times to close, or use a microwave-proof bowl and lid.

Cook in a microwave oven on high for about 2 minutes, or according to the manufacturer's instructions, until the sound of the popping kernels has stopped.

Transfer the popcorn to a large bowl. Spray the popcorn with olive oil, add the Parmesan, salt and parsley and toss until combined. Serve.

PER SERVING: 118 CALORIES, 2.61G FAT, 19.05G CARBS, 5.48G PROTEIN, 3.70G FIBRE, 89MG CALCIUM, 0.95MG IRON, 696MG SODIUM, 5µG FOLATE

chapter three
appetisers

craigie on main maine mussels

This contribution from Tony Maws, two-time James Beard Award-nominated chef and owner of the heralded restaurant Craigie on Main in Cambridge, Massachusetts is pure genius. Not only is it ridiculously easy and quick to prepare, but its broth is an exceptional diversion from white wine-based varieties. The dish is also a fine source of protein, iron, copper and selenium. Add some char-grilled crusty bread for dipping and you've found nirvana.

Serves 4

2 tablespoons extra-virgin olive oil
1 garlic clove, thinly sliced
12 live mussels (about 225g), cleaned and
   beards removed
pinch of coarse grey sea salt
pinch of dried chilli flakes
small pinch of high-quality saffron threads
1 teaspoon pastis
1 tablespoon sake
1½ teaspoons yellow miso paste
1½ teaspoons unsalted butter, softened
1 tablespoon vegetable stock
1 tablespoon roughly chopped fresh herbs
   (parsley, tarragon or chervil)
¾ teaspoon freshly squeezed lemon juice

Gently heat 1 tablespoon of the olive oil and the garlic in a heavy-based saucepan over a medium-high heat until the garlic toasts, becoming golden but not any darker. Remove the garlic with a slotted spoon and set aside.

Place the mussels in the infused olive oil and add the coarse grey sea salt, chilli flakes and saffron. Roast the mussels in the pan until they begin to open, then transfer them with the slotted spoon to a large bowl (discarding any that remain closed).

Deglaze the pan with the pastis and sake. Mix the miso and butter together and add it to the pan along with the vegetable stock and the reserved cooked garlic. Cook until the butter melts. Finish with the chopped herbs, lemon juice and the remaining 1 tablespoon of olive oil. Divide the sauce and mussels between 4 shallow bowls and serve.

PER SERVING: 124 CALORIES, 8.77G FAT, 3.16G CARBS, 6.10G PROTEIN, 0.25G FIBRE, 16MG CALCIUM, 2.09MG IRON, 304MG SODIUM, 23µG FOLATE

devilled egg salad bites

These irresistible two-bite crowd-pleasers are classics with a crunchy celery twist. They are also fast and easy sources of protein.

Serves 4

2 medium hard-boiled eggs, shelled and halved
1 tablespoon mayonnaise
⅛ teaspoon dry mustard powder
⅛ teaspoon sea salt
1 tablespoon finely chopped celery
paprika
½ teaspoon finely chopped chives (optional)

Carefully remove the yolks from the eggs, transfer to a small bowl and mash with the back of a fork until broken into small pieces. Stir in the mayonnaise, mustard powder and salt until well combined. Fold in the celery.

Scoop the mixture into the egg whites, sprinkle with paprika, and chives if you like, and serve.

PER SERVING: 62 CALORIES, 4.89G FAT, 0.30G CARBS, 3.19G PROTEIN, 0.05G FIBRE, 14MG CALCIUM, 0.48MG IRON, 127MG SODIUM, 12μG FOLATE

baked pot stickers

These tiny purses of seasoned pork and prawns are as good as those served in Chinese restaurants, but because they are baked instead of fried, they are far less greasy. If you don't have mini cupcake tins, fold the wonton wrappers tortellini-style and bake them on a baking tray.

Makes 24

225g lean pork mince
10 medium raw prawns, peeled and deveined
1 teaspoon finely chopped garlic
1 tablespoon peeled and finely chopped fresh ginger
3 tablespoons finely chopped spring onions
40g tinned, drained water chestnuts, finely chopped
1 medium egg yolk
2 teaspoons low-sodium soy sauce, plus extra to serve
1½ teaspoons rice wine vinegar
½ teaspoon unseasoned sesame oil
24 wonton wrappers
chilli sauce, to serve (optional)

Preheat the oven to 200°C/400°F/Gas Mark 6. Fill a small bowl with water.

Mix together all the ingredients except the wrappers and chilli sauce in a small bowl until well combined. Lay out a few wrappers on a flat surface (keep the rest covered with clingfilm). Place a heaped teaspoon of the filling in the centre of each wrapper. Lightly wet your fingers, then wet the edges of the wonton, pressing the edges together. Transfer, edges facing up, to 2 mini cupcake tins (or make 2 batches).

Bake for 10 minutes, or until the wonton juices are bubbling. Serve with extra soy sauce, and the chilli sauce, if you like.

PER POT STICKER: 55 CALORIES, 2.21G FAT, 5.03G CARBS, 3.09G PROTEIN, 0.21G FIBRE, 8MG CALCIUM, 0.47MG IRON, 69MG SODIUM, 9μG FOLATE

classic sushi hand rolls

While the potential of contracting listeria from raw fish causes many OB-GYNs to warn pregnant women against indulging in most options, not all sushi is off the table. You can easily and safely satisfy cravings by whipping up these hand rolls. You can also substitute other fillings, such as cooked asparagus, green beans, prawns, scallops or mango batons. Regardless, serve them with the expected accompaniments of soy sauce and wasabi (available in powder form).

Makes 6 hand rolls

140g sushi rice
225ml water
150g fresh or frozen crabmeat
1 tablespoon mayonnaise
2 tablespoons unseasoned rice wine vinegar
2 teaspoons granulated sugar
¾ teaspoon sea salt
3 nori sheets
¼ teaspoon toasted sesame seeds
6 cucumber batons, 3cm x 1cm
½ ripe Hass avocado, stoned, peeled and cut into 6 thin slices
soy sauce, to serve
wasabi, to serve

Rinse the rice multiple times until the water is clear. Drain and transfer to a saucepan with a tight-fitting lid. Add the water, place over a high heat and bring to the boil. Cover the pan, reduce the heat and simmer for 20 minutes.

Mix the crab and mayonnaise in a small bowl and set aside. In a separate small bowl, combine the vinegar, sugar and salt. Transfer the cooked rice to a large bowl and add the vinegar mixture. Gently mix with a rubber spatula. Cool the rice to just warm and cover with a clean, damp tea towel.

Cut the nori sheets in half horizontally. Lay 1 half down, with the short sides facing you, on a flat surface. Using moistened hands, gently press down one-sixth of the cooked rice onto the bottom half of the nori sheet. Sprinkle the rice with sesame seeds, top with a cucumber baton and add 1 thin slice of avocado and 1 tablespoon of the crab mixture. Holding the rice-covered part of the nori in the palm of your hand, fold the uncovered half of the nori over the filling(s) into a cone shape.

Repeat with the remaining ingredients until you have 6 hand rolls. Serve.

PER SERVING: 100 CALORIES, 4.50G FAT, 8.98G CARBS, 5.59G PROTEIN, 1.39G FIBRE, 31MG CALCIUM, 0.61MG IRON, 19MG SODIUM, 39µG FOLATE

balinese chicken satays with peanut sauce

Unlike ubiquitous 'satays', which consist of thinly sliced chicken on a skewer, this exotic Balinese-style starter is a mixture of chicken mince and Southeast Asian spices served on a lemongrass stalk. Note: if you can't find kaffir lime leaves, add half a bay leaf when cooking the spices, then remove it and add a generous pinch of lime zest when you add the coconut.

Serves 4

3 teaspoons rapeseed oil
1 tablespoon plus 1 teaspoon finely chopped garlic
¼ teaspoon dried chilli flakes
3½ teaspoons peeled and finely chopped fresh ginger
½ teaspoon ground turmeric
⅛ teaspoon ground white pepper
1 clove, crushed
½ teaspoon ground nutmeg
½ teaspoon ground coriander
sea salt
450g lean chicken mince
2 heaped tablespoons finely chopped shallots
1 kaffir lime leaf, finely shredded
20g grated fresh coconut or desiccated unsweetened coconut
freshly ground black pepper
4 lemongrass stalks, halved
2 heaped tablespoons finely chopped shallot
2 teaspoons soft light brown sugar
2 teaspoons freshly squeezed lime juice
130g smooth peanut butter
4 tablespoons water

Preheat the oven to 200°C/400°F/Gas Mark 6 and line a baking tray with baking parchment.

Heat 2 teaspoons of the oil in a small frying pan over a low heat. Add 1 tablespoon of garlic, a small pinch of the chilli flakes, 2 teaspoons of chopped ginger, the turmeric, white pepper, crushed clove, nutmeg, coriander and ½ teaspoon of salt, and fry for about 5 minutes until aromatic and cooked. Remove from the heat, leave to cool and transfer to a medium bowl. Mash to a paste with the back of a spoon, then mix in the chicken mince, shallots, lime leaf and coconut until completely combined. Season with salt and pepper.

Take an eighth of the chicken mixture and mould it around the top half of a lemongrass 'skewer' so that it is shaped like a long, thin ice lolly. Transfer to the lined baking sheet. Repeat with all the lemongrass and chicken mixture, making sure that they are evenly spaced on the baking sheet. Bake for 15–20 minutes, or until cooked through.

Meanwhile, make the peanut sauce. Heat the remaining 1 teaspoon of oil in a small frying pan over a medium heat until hot but not smoking. Add the shallot, the remaining 1 teaspoon of garlic and the remaining chilli flakes and ginger, and cook until aromatic.

Add the sugar, lime juice, peanut butter and water, and stir to combine, adding more water if the consistency is too thick. Transfer to a serving bowl and serve at room temperature alongside the cooked chicken skewers, or store, refrigerated and covered, for up to 3 days.

PER SERVING: 213 CALORIES, 14.91G FAT, 6.48G CARBS, 14.34G PROTEIN, 1.47G FIBRE, 18MG CALCIUM, 1.21MG IRON, 255MG SODIUM, 15µG FOLATE

chicken lettuce wraps

This classic and beloved Chinese appetiser is high in protein, low in carbs (which is good for anyone struggling with gestational diabetes) and a good source of potassium and vitamin D, thanks to the mushrooms. It's also as fun to eat as it is flavourful. Just serve the finely chopped chicken in a decorative bowl with a side of stacked lettuce leaves and let everyone build their own Asian-style burritos. Or make a batch for yourself and save the extra helpings for future snacking.

Serves 4

450g boneless, skinless chicken breasts
2 teaspoons vegetable oil
140g canned water chestnuts, drained
   and finely chopped
55g shiitake or chestnut mushrooms,
   diced
1 carrot, finely chopped
1 celery stick, finely chopped
1 tablespoon finely chopped garlic
2 tablespoons low-sodium soy sauce
2 tablespoons soft dark brown sugar
4 teaspoons seasoned rice wine vinegar
2 tablespoons sliced spring onions
8 large iceberg lettuce leaves

Preheat the oven to 180°C/350°F/Gas Mark 4. Rub the chicken breasts with 1 teaspoon of the oil and bake in an ovenproof frying pan for 30 minutes, or until cooked through. Carefully transfer the chicken to a plate to cool.

Add the remaining teaspoon of oil to the frying pan and heat on the hob over a medium heat until hot but not smoking, then add the water chestnuts, mushrooms, carrot, celery and garlic. Fry, stirring frequently, for 3 minutes. Finely chop the cooled chicken and add it to the vegetables.

Mix together the soy sauce, sugar and vinegar in a small bowl, add it to the chicken and vegetables and cook over a medium-high heat, stirring frequently, for 2 minutes. Transfer the mixture to a serving bowl and serve with a side stack of the lettuce leaves.

To eat, place a scoop of the chicken in the centre of a lettuce leaf, wrap the lettuce around its filling and enjoy!

PER SERVING: 207 CALORIES, 3.38G FAT, 14.31G CARBS, 28.14G PROTEIN, 2.60G FIBRE, 38MG CALCIUM, 1.68MG IRON, 367MG SODIUM, 26µG FOLATE

prawn, avocado and mango cocktail with coriander-lime dressing

If any recipe proves that elegance is all in the presentation, this one is it. Ridiculously quick to prepare, bright and fresh in flavour and colour and imparting potassium and vitamins C and B6, it becomes downright glamorous when served in a tumbler or cocktail glass.

Serves 4

2 teaspoons freshly squeezed lime juice
4 teaspoons extra-virgin olive oil
3 tablespoons chopped coriander, plus extra sprigs
   to garnish (optional)
¼ teaspoon runny honey
⅛ teaspoon sea salt
4 Cos lettuce leaves, sliced crossways into 2cm strips
½ Hass avocado, stoned, peeled and cubed
½ mango, stoned, peeled and cubed
12 peeled and deveined cooked prawns, chopped

Put the lime juice, olive oil, coriander, honey and salt in a blender and blend for 30 seconds, or until the coriander is puréed. Set aside.

Using 4 tumblers or Martini glasses, place a layer of lettuce in the base of each glass. Add a layer of avocado followed by a layer of mango. Top with the chopped prawns and a drizzle of the dressing. Garnish with coriander sprigs, if you like.

PER SERVING: 122 CALORIES, 8.17G FAT, 8.21G CARBS, 4.65G PROTEIN, 2.76G FIBRE, 24MG CALCIUM, 0.91MG IRON, 30MG SODIUM, 62µG FOLATE

aubergine caprese napoleons

So simple, so fresh and so good for you, this beautiful first course could easily act as a light lunch too. Just cook extra aubergine and store it in the fridge so that you can effortlessly make it anytime. Also, you can easily grill the aubergine instead of barbecuing it; place it on a grill pan – not too close to the heat source – and grill both sides, watching carefully that it doesn't burn.

Serves 4

1 large aubergine
¼ teaspoon sea salt, plus extra to serve
2 tablespoons olive oil
1 garlic clove, crushed or finely chopped
1 large heirloom or other flavourful ripe
    tomato, cut into 4 slices
115g pasteurised buffalo mozzarella
    cheese, cut into 4 slices
4 tablespoons balsamic vinegar
small handful of basil leaves
freshly ground black pepper

Preheat a gas barbecue. Slice off the top and bottom of the aubergine and cut into 8 slices. Season with the salt and leave to stand for 10 minutes.

Mix together the olive oil and garlic in a small bowl. Using a basting brush or spoon, brush the aubergine with the garlic oil. Cook the aubergine for about 8 minutes, or until golden on both sides.

Arrange 4 aubergine discs on a serving platter. Top with a layer of tomato, a layer of mozzarella and a final layer of aubergine. Set aside.

Bring the vinegar to the boil in a small saucepan over a medium-high heat and cook for about 4 minutes until reduced to a syrup, watching carefully not to burn it. Carefully drizzle the syrup over the 4 napoleons, adding extra drops on the platter for decoration. Sprinkle the basil atop the stacks and around the platter, and sprinkle with salt and ground pepper and serve.

PER SERVING: 206 CALORIES, 13.44G FAT, 13.29G CARBS, 8.08G PROTEIN, 5.24G FIBRE, 187MG CALCIUM, 0.72MG IRON, 271MG SODIUM, 40µG FOLATE

stewed tomato and white bean bruschetta

The secret to the full, rustic deliciousness of this Italian-style appetiser is in the sauce, so be sure to use vine-ripened tomatoes (ideally in summertime) for optimal flavour. Also, there's no need to wait for dinner guests to make this recipe. If you refrigerate the sauce, you can return to it for single servings whenever you want to adorn a piece of toast.

Serves 4

1 tablespoon extra-virgin olive oil
2 garlic cloves, peeled
2 large vine-ripened tomatoes, peeled, cut into 6 pieces and deseeded
generous pinch of dried chilli flakes
½ teaspoon sea salt
generous pinch of freshly ground black pepper
4 heaped tablespoons chopped fresh basil
190g tinned cannellini or haricot beans, rinsed and drained
4 thin slices of crusty Italian bread or 8 thin slices of baguette
40g pasteurised feta cheese, crumbled

Heat the olive oil in a wide pan over a medium-high heat. Crush 1 garlic clove and add to the pan with the tomatoes, chilli flakes, salt and pepper. Cook for 5 minutes, or until the tomatoes start to soften.

Crush the tomatoes with a potato masher. Continue cooking for about 10–15 minutes until the tomatoes become a thick sauce and there is very little liquid remaining. Stir in the basil and beans.

Meanwhile, preheat the grill. Rub 1 side of each slice of bread with the rest of the garlic clove. Grill the bread, garlic-side up, until golden. Top with the bean and tomato mixture and crumbled feta, and grill for about 5 minutes until hot, watching to make sure it doesn't burn.

Serve warm or at room temperature.

PER SERVING: 139 CALORIES, 5.74G FAT, 16.54G CARBS, 5.94G PROTEIN, 3.77G FIBRE, 91MG CALCIUM, 1.44MG IRON, 458MG SODIUM, 70µG FOLATE

chapter four

soups & salads

gazpacho with prawns

When invited to contribute a pregnancy-friendly dish for this book, Washington DC's famed chef José Andrés forwarded this recipe, an adaptation of his wife Patricia Fernandez de la Cruz's gazpacho. Loaded with fresh vegetables and topped with prawns, it's a light yet filling meal. And because it's served chilled, it's also soothing for the overheated mum-to-be.

Serves 4

For the gazpacho
900g ripe tomatoes, peeled, deseeded
   and diced
½ cucumber, peeled, deseeded and diced
½ green pepper, deseeded and diced
225ml water
6 tablespoons extra-virgin olive oil, plus
   extra for drizzling
2 tablespoons sherry vinegar
1–1½ slices of bread, torn into small pieces
½ teaspoon sea salt

For the prawns
12 large raw prawns, peeled and deveined
1 tablespoon olive oil
pinch of sea salt

For the garnish
4 slices of bread, 1cm thick, cut into
   1cm cubes
1 tablespoon olive oil
4 plum tomatoes, peeled, deseeded
   and diced
½ cucumber, peeled, deseeded and diced
½ red pepper, deseeded and diced
½ green pepper, deseeded and diced
1 tablespoon diced shallot
1 tablespoon finely chopped chives
sea salt, for sprinkling

Put all the gazpacho ingredients in a blender or food processor and blend until very smooth, adding more water if necessary. Strain through a fine-mesh sieve, cover and chill.

Prepare the prawns: heat the oil in a large frying pan over a medium-high heat. Cut the prawns lengthways about halfway down so that they open into a 'Y' shape (this allows the prawns to cook more evenly). Once the oil is hot, cook the prawns for 2–3 minutes. Set aside.

Preheat the oven to 180°C/350°F/Gas Mark 4. Put the bread cubes in a mixing bowl, drizzle with the oil and toss to coat evenly. Spread the bread cubes in a single layer on a baking tray and bake for 15–20 minutes until golden, turning once or twice with a fish slice. Leave to cool.

Mix together the plum tomatoes, cucumber, red and green peppers and shallot in a bowl.

To serve, place 3 prawns in the centre of 4 soup bowls. Arrange some of the tomato-cucumber mixture around the edge. Sprinkle with the chives and sea salt and top with some croutons. Drizzle with a little extra-virgin olive oil. Pour the chilled gazpacho into a jug. Set the bowls in front of your guests and serve the gazpacho at the table.

PER SERVING: 384 CALORIES, 28.55G FAT, 22.68G CARBS, 9.53G PROTEIN, 5.16G FIBRE, 68MG CALCIUM, 2.32MG IRON, 426MG SODIUM, 90µG FOLATE

decadent chicken soup

Chicken soup is not only delicious and nutritious, but also aids in curing colds and flu – a perk for someone who's steering clear of medications for the sake of her unborn baby. The addition of onion to this dish gives it a richness reminiscent of French onion soup (minus the calories) and the veggies impart added nutritional benefit. Double the recipe and freeze it for future consumption.

Serves 4

1.4 litres water
½ chicken on the bone, cut into pieces
2 onions, unpeeled
1 parsnip, peeled
1 swede, peeled and quartered
1 large turnip, peeled and quartered
sea salt and freshly ground black pepper
½ courgette, diced
½ carrot, peeled and diced

Put the water and chicken in a large saucepan and bring to the boil. Skim off any white froth that rises to the top. Add the onions, parsnip, swede and turnip, cover and simmer for at least 2½ hours.

Remove from the heat and leave to cool. Remove the chicken, discard the vegetables and strain the stock into a clean saucepan.

Remove and discard the skin and bones from the chicken, cut the meat into bite-sized chunks and add to the stock. Season with salt and pepper, then bring to the boil. Add the courgette and carrot, and simmer for 10 minutes, or until the vegetables are cooked but still firm. Serve hot.

PER SERVING: 135 CALORIES, 1.45G FAT, 23.46G CARBS, 8.30G PROTEIN, 6.28G FIBRE, 102MG CALCIUM, 1.29MG IRON, 90MG SODIUM, 68µG FOLATE

hot and sour chicken and prawn soup

The genius of this Thai-style soup is that it's lightning-fast to prepare and amazingly light, yet boldly flavourful. It's also quite flexible. Skip the chicken, prawns or both, or add broccoli, pak choi or spinach. The number of combinations is limited only by your imagination and fridge contents. Bonus: the soup's spices can help clear pregnancy-related congestion.

Serves 4

1.4 litres chicken stock
350g boneless, skinless chicken breasts, thinly sliced into
    2 x 2.5cm strips
12 medium raw prawns, peeled and deveined
115g chestnut or other mushrooms, sliced
2 tablespoons thinly sliced lemongrass stalks
2 tablespoons peeled and finely chopped fresh ginger
1–2 fresh bird's eye or other hot chilli, finely chopped
3–4 tablespoons Thai fish sauce, or to taste
3 tablespoons freshly squeezed lime juice, or to taste

Bring the chicken stock to the boil in a large saucepan. Add the chicken, prawns, mushrooms, lemongrass, ginger and chilli, and cook for about 3 minutes, or until the chicken is just cooked through.

Season the soup with the fish sauce and lime juice, adding more if you like.

Ladle into 4 bowls and serve.

PER SERVING: 272 CALORIES, 5.21G FAT, 18.42G CARBS, 35.11G PROTEIN, 0.92G FIBRE, 39MG CALCIUM, 2.71MG IRON, 1353MG SODIUM, 32µG FOLATE

mexican-style bean and vegetable soup

If you're craving Mexican food, don't reach for fast-food tacos. Instead, try this soup. Its spices conjure up the flavour of seasoned beef mince and the beans add heartiness (and much-needed fibre and protein). But its light, vegetarian nature means it's far better for you.

Serves 6

2 x 15cm corn tortillas
1.4 litres chicken or vegetable stock
425g tinned pinto beans, rinsed and drained
425g tinned black beans, rinsed and drained
425g tinned sweetcorn, rinsed and drained
2 medium courgettes, quartered lengthways and cut into slices
¾ teaspoon dried oregano
½ teaspoon ground cumin
¾ teaspoon paprika
¼ teaspoon chilli powder
⅛ teaspoon dried chilli flakes
½ teaspoon sea salt
1 teaspoon freshly squeezed lime juice plus 1 lime, cut into 6 wedges
55g Cheddar cheese, grated (optional)

Preheat the oven to 180°C/350°F/Gas Mark 4. Slice the tortillas into long, thin triangles. Spread in a single layer on a baking tray and bake for 20 minutes, or until crisp. Leave to cool.

Combine the stock, beans, sweetcorn, courgettes, oregano, spices and salt in a large saucepan. Bring to the boil, then reduce to a simmer and cook for 5 minutes. Stir in the lime juice.

Ladle the soup into 6 bowls and top with the tortilla strips and cheese, if using. Serve with a lime wedge on the side.

PER SERVING: 345 CALORIES, 6.97G FAT, 52.38G CARBS, 20.75G PROTEIN, 12.22G FIBRE, 140MG CALCIUM, 3.83MG IRON, 887MG SODIUM, 228µG FOLATE

carrot and ginger soup

Easy to prepare and perfect for a light lunch, dinner or between-meal snack, this recipe by New York food writer and chef Lisa Roberts-Lehan offers comfort in the form of stomach-settling ginger. It also boasts vitamin K-rich carrots, as well as leeks, onions and garlic, which reduce 'bad' cholesterol.

Serves 4

3 tablespoons olive oil
1 small onion, diced
1 leek, white part only, chopped
2 tablespoons peeled and thinly sliced fresh ginger, or to taste
2 garlic cloves, chopped
1 litre vegetable stock
225ml semi-skimmed milk or unsweetened almond milk
9–12 medium carrots, peeled and chopped
½ teaspoon sea salt
freshly ground black pepper

Heat the oil in a large saucepan over a medium heat. Add the onion, leek, ginger and garlic, and sauté, stirring, for 1–2 minutes. Add the stock, milk and carrots and season to taste. Bring to a simmer and cook for about 20–30 minutes, or until the carrots are tender.

Remove the pan from the heat and leave the soup to cool for 3–5 minutes. Transfer the soup to a blender or food processor and blend until smooth, adding more water if needed. Once all the soup is blended, return to the pan and simmer to reheat.

PER SERVING: 221 CALORIES, 10.86G FAT, 27.85G CARBS, 4.34G PROTEIN, 5.34G FIBRE, 145MG CALCIUM, 1.38MG IRON, 1367MG SODIUM, 50µG FOLATE

chopped vegetable salad with avocado and parmesan

San Francisco chef David Gingrass garnered legions of fans with this simple, yet wholly satisfying and abundantly healthy salad. Add roasted chicken for extra protein and substance.

Serves 4

1 small shallot, finely chopped
½ teaspoon Dijon mustard
1 tablespoon sherry wine vinegar
2 tablespoons extra-virgin olive oil, plus extra for the salad
sea salt and freshly ground black pepper
½ ripe avocado, stoned, peeled and diced
165g fresh sweetcorn kernels (or other sweet vegetable in season, such as peas, broad beans or courgettes)
½ small red onion, diced
35g blanched carrot, diced
30g celery heart, diced
70g deseeded and diced cucumber
45g mixed salad leaves, chopped
75g cherry tomatoes, halved
25g Parmesan cheese, freshly grated

Put the shallot, mustard and vinegar in a small bowl and mix well. Whisk in the olive oil and then season to taste with salt and pepper.

Combine the avocado, sweetcorn, onion, carrot, celery, cucumber, salad leaves and tomatoes in a serving bowl. Add the vinaigrette and toss well. Season to taste with salt and pepper and sprinkle with the Parmesan. Divide between 4 serving plates and serve.

PER SERVING: 170 CALORIES, 11.87G FAT, 13.23G CARBS, 4.34G PROTEIN, 3.46G FIBRE, 84MG CALCIUM, 0.70MG IRON, 119MG SODIUM, 52µG FOLATE

apple and celery salad with currants and champagne vinaigrette

This elegant mélange of fruit, vegetables and almonds can be an outstanding side salad or main course, especially if you add roasted chicken.

Serves 4

1 tablespoon champagne vinegar
1 teaspoon finely chopped shallot
freshly ground black pepper
¼ teaspoon sea salt
½ teaspoon granulated sugar
⅛ teaspoon Dijon mustard
2 tablespoons rapeseed oil
1 crisp red apple, cored and thinly sliced
70g toasted almonds, halved
4 celery sticks, sliced into 1cm pieces
20g currants
280g Cos lettuce hearts, chopped

Put the vinegar, shallot, pepper to taste, salt, sugar and mustard in a small non-reactive bowl and whisk until blended. Whisk in the oil to combine and set aside.

Combine the apple, almonds, celery, currants and lettuce in a salad bowl. Add the dressing, toss and serve.

PER SERVING: 219 CALORIES, 15.52G FAT, 17.13G CARBS, 5.28G PROTEIN, 5.56G FIBRE, 91MG CALCIUM, 1.80MG IRON, 185MG SODIUM, 117µG FOLATE

chinese chicken salad

watermelon, rocket, feta and mint salad

This crunchy, addictive salad with a hot dry mustard kick pays tribute to Wolfgang Puck's famed Chinois restaurant (the leader in Asian fusion food), as well as to the under-appreciated Chinese leaf. Also known as Chinese cabbage, it is low in calories and high in vitamin C and calcium. Bonus: the dressing's sesame oil is an antioxidant and rich in minerals and vitamins A, B and E.

This unexpected combination dances on the palate thanks to the sweetness of the watermelon, tartness of the lime, saltiness of the feta and olives, and semi-spicy herbaceous character of the rocket. Thanks to tummy-soothing watermelon, it can also be a godsend to the queasy mum. Note: if possible, drain the watermelon cubes (in a colander over a bowl) in the fridge beforehand.

Serves 4

30g flaked almonds
2 teaspoons dry mustard powder
2 tablespoons seasoned rice wine vinegar
1½ teaspoons low-sodium soy sauce
1 tablespoon light sesame oil
2 tablespoons rapeseed oil
generous pinch of coarse sea salt
½ teaspoon granulated sugar
freshly ground black pepper
225g Chinese leaves, shredded
75g deseeded and julienned red pepper
125g cooked chicken breast, shredded

Serves 4

½ small red onion, thinly sliced and halved
2 tablespoons freshly squeezed lime juice
1 tablespoon extra-virgin olive oil
6 Kalamata olives, stoned and chopped
225g ripe deseeded watermelon flesh, cut into thin triangles
30g rocket leaves
3 tablespoons chopped mint
50g pasteurised feta cheese, crumbled

Heat a small, dry frying pan over a medium heat, then add the almonds and toast, stirring constantly, for 2–3 minutes. Remove from the heat and set aside.

Combine the mustard, vinegar, soy sauce, sesame and rapeseed oils, salt, sugar and pepper to taste in a salad bowl and whisk until combined. Add the Chinese leaves, red pepper, chicken and almonds, and toss until evenly coated with the dressing. Serve.

Combine the onion, lime juice, olive oil and olives in a small serving bowl, and mix until combined and the onions are coated. Cover and leave to stand for 15 minutes.

Add the watermelon, rocket, mint and feta. Toss so that the dressing coats the rocket and then serve.

PER SERVING: 104 CALORIES, 6.53G FAT, 9.48G CARBS, 2.91G PROTEIN, 1.27G FIBRE, 99MG CALCIUM, 1.16MG IRON, 209MG SODIUM, 28µG FOLATE

PER SERVING: 219 CALORIES, 14.00G FAT, 5.46G CARBS, 16.68G PROTEIN, 1.40G FIBRE, 57MG CALCIUM, 1.62MG IRON, 276MG SODIUM, 49µG FOLATE

deluxe greek salad

If you love the cool, satisfying goodness that is Greek salad, you'll adore this adaptation of 'Barefoot Contessa' chef Ina Garten's version. It turns summertime's standby into a hearty side dish or main course, and provides much-needed vegetables and protein.

Serves 4

½ teaspoon finely chopped garlic
1 teaspoon dried oregano
¼ teaspoon Dijon mustard
1 tablespoon plus 1 teaspoon red wine vinegar
¼ teaspoon sea salt
pinch of freshly ground black pepper
3 tablespoons extra-virgin olive oil
1 red pepper, deseeded and chopped
2 plum or other vine-ripened tomatoes, deseeded and
    cut into 2.5cm cubes
1 cucumber, deseeded and cut into 2.5cm cubes
1 courgette, peeled and cut into 2.5cm cubes
1 large red onion, chopped
140g cooked chicken breast meat, cut into 2.5cm cubes
150g pasteurised feta cheese, crumbled
45g Kalamata olives, stoned and chopped
2 fresh flat-leaf parsley sprigs (optional)

Whisk together the garlic, oregano, mustard, vinegar, salt, pepper and olive oil in a large bowl until combined. Add the red pepper, tomatoes, cucumber, courgette, onion and chicken, and gently toss until all the chicken and vegetables are well coated.

Add the feta and olives and toss lightly. Cover and set aside for 30 minutes to allow the flavours to blend before garnishing with the parsley, if you like, and serving.

PER SERVING: 310 CALORIES, 18.74G FAT, 12.83G CARBS, 21.11G PROTEIN, 2.81G FIBRE, 236MG CALCIUM, 1.84MG IRON, 696MG SODIUM, 68µG FOLATE

spinach salad with shiitakes, pine nuts and lemon dressing

A tart, light lemon dressing is the perfect partner for sautéed shiitake mushrooms and toasted pine nuts. Feel free to add a tablespoon of crumbled feta for visual contrast and creamy deliciousness, or throw in some chopped, cooked bacon for the ultimate decadence.

Serves 4

1 teaspoon olive oil
125g fresh shiitake mushrooms, sliced
20g pine nuts
2 tablespoons rapeseed oil
4½ teaspoons freshly squeezed lemon juice
⅛ teaspoon sea salt
pinch of freshly ground black pepper
150g spinach leaves, stalks removed (prepared weight)

Heat the olive oil in a small frying pan over a medium heat until it is hot but not smoking. Add the mushrooms and sauté, stirring frequently, for about 4 minutes, or until lightly browned. Set aside.

In a separate small frying pan over a medium heat, toast the pine nuts, stirring frequently, for about 5 minutes. Leave to cool.

Put the rapeseed oil, lemon juice and salt and pepper in a serving bowl and stir with a fork until completely combined. Add the spinach, mushrooms and pine nuts, and toss together thoroughly before serving.

PER SERVING: 113 CALORIES, 10.48G FAT, 3.52G CARBS, 2.09G PROTEIN, 1.47G FIBRE, 40MG CALCIUM, 1.29MG IRON, 106MG SODIUM, 78µG FOLATE

courgette and lamb's lettuce with lemon and parmesan

Courgette takes on a whole new – and perhaps surprisingly tasty – personality when served raw, shaved into paper-thin ribbons and drizzled with lemon juice and olive oil. Plus, it's a good source of vitamin C and dietary fibre.

Serves 4

3 medium courgettes, peeled
115g Parmesan cheese, plus extra for sprinkling
85g lamb's lettuce (corn salad)
2 tablespoons extra-virgin olive oil
2 teaspoons freshly squeezed lemon juice
sea salt and freshly ground black pepper
1 tablespoon finely chopped flat-leaf parsley

Using a vegetable peeler, shave the courgettes lengthways into long ribbons. Then shave the Parmesan into long ribbons. Transfer both to a serving bowl and add the lamb's lettuce.

Whisk together the olive oil and lemon juice in a small bowl and pour it over the salad.

Season to taste with salt and pepper and toss lightly, then sprinkle with extra Parmesan and the parsley, and serve.

PER SERVING: 197 CALORIES, 13.75G FAT, 6.48G CARBS, 12.21G PROTEIN, 1.82G FIBRE, 374MG CALCIUM, 0.99MG IRON, 471MG SODIUM, 55µG FOLATE

roasted beetroot, orange and avocado salad

Colourful and loaded with folate, vitamin C and 'good fats', this salad also has wonderful texture thanks to hearty beetroot, melt-in-your-mouth avocado and juicy orange slices.

Serves 4

2 medium beetroots, tops removed
2 tablespoons rapeseed oil
2 tablespoons balsamic or champagne vinegar
1 tablespoon freshly squeezed orange juice
½ teaspoon sea salt
freshly ground black pepper
1 ripe orange, peeled
½ ripe but firm avocado, stoned, peeled and cubed
45g lamb's lettuce (corn salad) or baby salad leaves (optional)
40g pasteurised feta cheese, crumbled

Preheat the oven to 200°C/400°F/Gas Mark 6. Line a baking dish with foil and place the beetroot on top. Drizzle with 1 tablespoon of the oil and 1 tablespoon of the vinegar. Cover tightly with more foil and roast for 45 minutes. Remove from the oven and set aside to cool.

Put the remaining 1 tablespoon of oil and 1 tablespoon of vinegar in a small bowl with the orange juice, season to taste and whisk until combined.

Once the beetroots have cooled, peel them with a knife, cut into 4cm cubes and transfer to a serving bowl.

Slice the orange in half and cut out the segments. Add them to the serving bowl along with the avocado and salad leaves, if using. Drizzle the dressing over, toss to coat and then sprinkle the feta on top before serving.

PER SERVING: 129 CALORIES, 8.72G FAT, 10.53G CARBS, 2.90G PROTEIN, 3.50G FIBRE, 74MG CALCIUM, 0.68MG IRON, 430MG SODIUM, 80µG FOLATE

chapter five

main courses

mushroom quinoa risotto

If you're not yet on board with the recent (and ironically ancient)
trend of cooking with quinoa, this guiltlessly decadent recipe is
your incentive. Created by cooking instructor, cookbook author
and mother of three Dana Slatkin, it elevates the grain known for
its simultaneously soft and crunchy character to gourmet status.
The benefits beyond flavour are great: quinoa is an exceptional
source of protein, calcium, iron and all eight essential amino acids!
Tip: before using quinoa, rinse it once or twice under cold water to
remove the slightly bitter residue. Garnish with chives for visual flair.

Serves 4

700ml mushroom or chicken stock
1 tablespoon plus 2 teaspoons olive oil
2 tablespoons finely chopped shallot
1 teaspoon finely chopped garlic
250g quinoa, rinsed in a sieve
   under cold water
125ml dry white wine
225g fresh shiitake or closed cup
   mushrooms, diced
sea salt and freshly ground black pepper
225g oyster mushrooms, sliced
35g Parmesan cheese, freshly grated,
   plus extra shavings to serve

Heat the stock in a medium saucepan over a low heat and simmer while you
prepare the rest of the dish.

Heat the 1 tablespoon of oil in a separate medium saucepan over a medium heat.
Add the shallot and garlic, and cook until soft and translucent, stirring frequently to
prevent browning. Add the quinoa and cook for about 3 minutes, stirring, until the
grains are coated in oil and fragrant.

Add the wine and cook, stirring occasionally, until evaporated. Ladle 125ml of the
hot stock into the quinoa, stir and simmer for about 3 minutes, or until the liquid has
evaporated. Continue the process, adding 125ml of stock at a time, until the quinoa
is fully cooked and there is no more stock – this will take about 25 minutes.

Meanwhile, heat the remaining 2 teaspoons of oil in a small frying pan and cook
the shiitake mushrooms until browned. Season to taste with salt and pepper,
transfer to a bowl and set aside. Repeat with the oyster mushrooms.

Stir the shiitake mushrooms and Parmesan into the risotto. Spoon into 4 serving
bowls and top with the oyster mushrooms. Serve immediately, with additional
Parmesan shavings for sprinkling.

PER SERVING: 386 CALORIES, 11.43G FAT, 47.55G CARBS, 17.95G PROTEIN, 5.39G FIBRE, 152 MG CALCIUM,
4.12MG IRON, 553MG SODIUM, 141μG FOLATE

vegetarian chilli

Filling and loaded with healthy ingredients, this classic is best garnished with grated Cheddar, spring onions, diced avocado, a dollop of yogurt or soured cream or finely chopped fresh coriander. Freeze leftovers for an effortless future meal over a bowl of rice.

Serves 4

2 tablespoons rapeseed oil
2 large onions, chopped
2 large red peppers, deseeded and roughly chopped
2 tablespoons chopped garlic
2 tablespoons chilli powder
2 teaspoons dried oregano
2 teaspoons ground cumin
1/8 teaspoon cayenne pepper
850g tinned chilli beans, drained
125ml water
360g peeled, diced tomatoes with juices
165g sweetcorn kernels
250g courgettes, cubed
1 teaspoon sea salt

Heat the oil in a large heavy saucepan over a medium-high heat. Add the onions, red peppers and garlic, and sauté for about 10 minutes until the onions are soft. Add the spices and stir to combine. Mix in the beans, water and the tomatoes. Bring to the boil, stirring occasionally, then reduce the heat to medium-low and simmer for 10 minutes. Stir in the sweetcorn, courgettes and salt, and then simmer for a further 5 minutes.

Ladle the chilli into serving bowls and serve with any of the embellishments mentioned above.

PER SERVING: 428 CALORIES, 10.15G FAT, 70.76G CARBS, 19.55G PROTEIN, 21.58G FIBRE, 195MG CALCIUM, 7.01MG IRON, 1663MG SODIUM, 190µG FOLATE

red snapper with vinaigrette provençal

Red snapper is a fish that is low in mercury, and thus safe to consume in moderation while pregnant. An excellent source of protein, omega-3 fatty acids and vitamins B6 and B12, it's also a deliciously light partner for the vibrant, tangy flavours of the accompanying vinaigrette.

Serves 4

10g unsalted butter
2 small onions, finely chopped
1 tablespoon finely chopped garlic
3 tablespoons sherry vinegar
1 medium tomato, deseeded and chopped
½ medium red pepper, deseeded and finely chopped
2 tablespoons olive oil
1 tablespoon finely chopped flat-leaf parsley
1 tablespoon finely chopped stoned Kalamata olives
sea salt and freshly ground black pepper
4 x 175g red snapper fillets

Heat the butter in a large frying pan over a medium heat and cook the onions and garlic, stirring frequently, for about 10 minutes until the onions are translucent.

Add the vinegar and tomato and cook, covered, for 5 minutes. Add the red pepper and olive oil and cook, stirring, for 2 minutes. Stir in the parsley and olives and season to taste. Transfer to a bowl and set aside.

Season the fish to taste, add to the same hot frying pan, in batches if necessary, and cook over a medium heat for 3 minutes per side. Transfer the fish to 4 serving plates. Warm the vinaigrette in the pan, stirring, then spoon onto each piece of fish and serve.

PER SERVING: 163 CALORIES, 9.14G FAT, 6.28G CARBS, 12.59G PROTEIN, 1.34G FIBRE, 37MG CALCIUM, 0.55MG IRON, 59MG SODIUM, 20µG FOLATE

grilled sake-marinated salmon fillet in shiso broth

Napa Valley's James Beard Award-winning chef, Hiro Sone, is one of the best chefs in the United States, and this recipe proves the point. Light and easy to prepare, its elegance and complex flavours exude four-star quality – as well as pregnancy essentials such as protein and omega-3s from the salmon, and calcium, folic acid, vitamins C and K, iron and fibre from the spinach. If you can't find the exotic herb known as shiso, simply skip it and the dish will still elicit a lifelong love affair.

Serves 4

2 tablespoons dry sake
4 tablespoons soy sauce
2 tablespoons mirin
3 tablespoons granulated sugar
1/8 teaspoon peeled and grated fresh ginger
1/8 teaspoon grated garlic
4 x 175g salmon fillets, about 2.5cm thick (preferably wild salmon)
475ml chicken stock or water
1/2 teaspoon rice wine vinegar
85g shiitake mushrooms, stems removed and sliced (prepared weight)
180g spinach leaves
1 spring onion, thinly sliced
2 shiso leaves, sliced (optional)
1 teaspoon toasted sesame seeds

Whisk together the sake, soy sauce, mirin, sugar, ginger and garlic in a small bowl. Reserve 3 tablespoons of this marinade but use the rest to marinate the salmon, covered and refrigerated, for at least 3 hours or overnight.

Preheat the grill to high. Rinse the marinade off the salmon and pat dry. Lay the salmon on the grill pan or a baking sheet, place under the grill and cook for about 10 minutes until the surface turns a nice mahogany colour.

Meanwhile, combine the stock, reserved sake marinade, vinegar and mushrooms in a medium saucepan and bring to the boil. Add the spinach and spring onion and return to the boil.

Divide the stock and vegetables between 4 serving bowls and sprinkle with the shiso, if using. Place 1 salmon fillet in the middle of each bowl, sprinkle with a few sesame seeds and serve.

PER SERVING: 175 CALORIES, 3.68G FAT, 20.94G CARBS, 13.36G PROTEIN, 2.82G FIBRE, 88MG CALCIUM, 2.97MG IRON, 1276MG SODIUM, 126µG FOLATE

sautéed salmon with green beans, tomatoes and sherry vinaigrette

Salmon is one of the best types of fish you can eat while pregnant due to its high amount of protein and omega-3 fatty acids, the latter of which are essential for a baby's brain development. This elegant dish is big on flavour and low on effort and calories. What else could a hungry pregnant woman ask for – except, perhaps, someone else to prepare it for her.

Serves 4

4 tablespoons plus 2 teaspoons extra-virgin olive oil
2 tablespoons sherry vinegar
1½ teaspoons finely chopped shallot
1 teaspoon sea salt
20 cherry or grape tomatoes, halved
425g green beans, trimmed
4 x 115g salmon fillets (preferably wild salmon)
sea salt and freshly ground black pepper

Put the 4 tablespoons of olive oil, the vinegar, shallot and salt in a small bowl and stir to combine. Add the tomatoes, stir to coat and set aside.

Bring a large saucepan of water to the boil and blanch the green beans for about 3 minutes so that they still retain a slight crunch. Quickly transfer the beans to a bowl of iced water to cool, then drain.

Heat the remaining 2 teaspoons of oil in a large frying pan over a medium-high heat. Generously sprinkle the salmon with salt and pepper, then add to the pan, in batches if necessary, and cook for about 4 minutes per side, or until brown and crisp on the outside and just cooked through on the inside. Transfer to serving plates and keep warm.

Add the tomatoes, vinaigrette and green beans to the hot pan and cook for 2–3 minutes or until the tomatoes begin to soften. Pour over the salmon and serve.

PER SERVING: 380 CALORIES, 24.05G FAT, 11.41G CARBS, 26.94G PROTEIN, 4.76G FIBRE, 56MG CALCIUM, 2.05MG IRON, 646MG SODIUM, 58µG FOLATE

miso-marinated black cod with japanese-style steamed spinach and edamame

This spin on famed Japanese chef Nobu Matsuhisa's rich miso-marinated black cod is elegant enough to serve to dinner guests and easy enough to prepare for a midweek meal. The densely flavoured fish, coated with a light sweet and savoury glaze, together with iron-rich steamed spinach is a winning and wholly addictive combination, while the edamame adds whimsically decorative nibbles to the dish, but can be easily skipped if desired.

Serves 4

2 tablespoons sake
2 tablespoons mirin
135g yellow miso paste
50g plus 2 tablespoons granulated sugar
4 x 150g black cod or sea bass fillets
350g baby spinach leaves
3 tablespoons sesame seeds
2½ tablespoons soy sauce
40g cooked, shelled fresh or frozen edamame beans, to garnish

Bring the sake and mirin to the boil in a medium saucepan over a high heat. Boil for 20 seconds to evaporate the alcohol. Remove from the heat, add the miso paste and the 50g of sugar and stir until combined. Leave to cool.

Place the fish in a single layer in a container with a tight-sealing cover. Generously coat each piece of fish with the miso mixture, cover and refrigerate overnight or up to 30 hours.

Preheat the grill to high.

Wipe off, but don't rinse, all of the miso sauce from the fish. Transfer to the grill pan or a baking sheet and grill until the fish caramelises to a light brown. Turn off the grill and turn the oven to 200°C/400°F/Gas Mark 6. Bake for 10–15 minutes.

Fill a large saucepan with 2.5cm of water and fit the pan with a steamer. Bring the water to the boil. Place the spinach in the steamer, in batches if necessary, cover and steam the spinach for 2 minutes, or until wilted. Remove the spinach, drain and leave to cool. Squeeze any excess water out of the spinach, roughly chop and set aside.

Toast the sesame seeds in a dry frying pan over a high heat for about 2 minutes, or until light brown. Using a coffee grinder or food processor, grind the seeds. Add the remaining 2 tablespoons of sugar and grind until the mixture becomes a paste. Add the soy sauce and blend.

Combine the spinach and sesame seed dressing thoroughly in a bowl. Serve alongside the fish, garnished with the edamame beans.

PER SERVING: 168 CALORIES, 2.55G FAT, 8.82 CARBS, 26.24G PROTEIN, 3.04G FIBRE, 136MG CALCIUM, 3.66MG IRON, 944MG SODIUM, 201µG FOLATE

tacolicious fish tacos

If anyone knows how to do tacos right, it's San Francisco's Tacolicious. The restaurant focuses squarely on exciting ingredients, expertly prepared and neatly tucked into warm tortillas. This recipe – a home cook-friendly version of one of their specials – underscores their expertise. A combination of light, spice-spiked fish, tangy Greek yogurt and lime-kissed coleslaw, it can be devoured with the confidence that your meal is not only delicious but also a good source of protein and vitamins C, B6, B12 and K.

Serves 4

2 teaspoons ground dried ancho chilli
1 teaspoon ground chipotle chilli
 or chilli powder
1 teaspoon garlic powder
1 teaspoon dried oregano
1½ teaspoons sea salt
450g cod fillet, cut into 5cm pieces
125ml Greek yogurt
1 teaspoon ground cumin
6 teaspoons freshly squeezed lime juice
140g cabbage, shredded
2–3 radishes, thinly sliced
4 tablespoons chopped coriander
1 tablespoon olive oil
8 x 13–15cm corn or flour tortillas
1 avocado, stoned, peeled and chopped

Mix together the ground chilli, garlic powder, oregano and ½ teaspoon of salt in a small bowl. Season the fish with a light sprinkle of this popular Mexican blend of 'ancho recado' spices and set aside.

Put the yogurt, cumin, 2 teaspoons of the lime juice and ½ teaspoon of the salt in a small non-reactive bowl and mix well, then cover and refrigerate. In a separate non-reactive bowl, mix together the cabbage, radishes, coriander and the remaining 4 teaspoons of lime juice and ½ teaspoon of salt, and set aside.

Heat the olive oil in a cast-iron or non-stick frying pan and cook the fish for about 2–3 minutes per side.

Warm the tortillas by wrapping them in foil and heating them in a warm oven.

To assemble, place some avocado and a piece of fish in the centre of each tortilla, and top with 1 tablespoon of the yogurt mixture and some of the cabbage-radish coleslaw.

PER SERVING: 326 CALORIES, 12.17G FAT, 28.88G CARBS, 26.23G PROTEIN, 7.85G FIBRE, 149MG CALCIUM, 2.22MG IRON, 1006MG SODIUM, 76µG FOLATE

curried scallops with smoky lentils

These lentils, inspired by a recipe in the divine *Summertime Anytime Cookbook*, are an excellent source of dietary fibre and iron while scallops are superb providers of protein, vitamin B12, phosphorus and selenium. Married with bacon and curry powder, they are a direct route to dinnertime divinity. Tip: to finely chop the bacon, partially freeze it, then cut it before it thaws.

Serves 4

2 rashers of thick-cut nitrate-free
    streaky bacon, finely chopped
150g green or black lentils
1 large shallot, finely chopped
45g carrot, diced
2 tablespoons diced celery
300ml low-sodium chicken stock
sea salt and freshly ground black pepper
2 tablespoons curry powder
12 large scallops, shelled and cleaned
1 tablespoon rapeseed oil

Cook the bacon in a small saucepan over a medium heat until it just begins to brown. Add the lentils, shallot, carrot and celery. Stir to coat with the bacon fat and cook for about 2 minutes. Add the chicken stock, then simmer, uncovered and stirring occasionally, for about 30 minutes until the lentils are soft. Season with a generous pinch of salt and pepper to taste.

Meanwhile, mix the curry powder with generous pinches of salt and pepper on a plate and dredge the scallops in the curry mixture, then set aside.

Heat the oil in a large frying pan until hot but not smoking. Brown the scallops on each side for 2–3 minutes.

To serve, divide the cooked lentils between 4 serving plates and top with 3 curried scallops.

PER SERVING: 252 CALORIES, 6.04G FAT, 28.47G CARBS, 20.63G PROTEIN, 12.48G FIBRE, 59MG CALCIUM, 4.20MG IRON, 277MG SODIUM, 192µG FOLATE

fast and fabulous paella

Napa Valley's Zuzu restaurant is beloved for its paella. This adaptation, based on original chef Charles Weber's exceptional and far more complicated recipe, pays tribute to the flavour minus the labour. It's also high in protein plus vitamin C from the red pepper. Tips: ask your butcher to halve the baby back ribs crossways so that they are bite-sized when you cook and serve them, or swap them for slices of chicken breast if you like. And don't forget the safe-shellfish rule of thumb: if its shell doesn't open up during cooking, don't eat it because it could make you sick. You can also skip the shellfish and the dish will still deliver.

Serves 4

350ml chicken stock
125ml vegetable juice
½ small onion, chopped
½ large red pepper, deseeded and chopped
3 garlic cloves, peeled
1 bay leaf
pinch of saffron threads
450g baby back ribs (pork loin ribs), halved
¼ teaspoon coarse sea salt, or to taste
2 teaspoons olive oil
150g paella rice
65g frozen green peas
50g cured chorizo, diced
8 large raw prawns, peeled and deveined
8 live clams
8 live mussels

Combine the chicken stock, vegetable juice, onion, red pepper, 2 of the garlic cloves, bay leaf and saffron in a medium saucepan and bring to the boil. Slice the ribs into individual riblets and add them to the pan. Reduce to a simmer and cook for 20 minutes. Stir in the salt, taste, and add more if needed and leave to cool. Remove and discard the bay leaf and set aside the ribs.

Transfer the liquid to a blender and blend until combined.

Preheat the oven to 230°C/450°F/Gas Mark 8. Slice the remaining garlic clove thinly. Heat the olive oil in a large ovenproof frying pan over a medium heat. Add the sliced garlic and sauté for 2 minutes. Add the paella rice, stir to coat and scatter evenly around the base of the pan.

Arrange the ribs, in a single layer, evenly on top of the rice. Scatter the peas and chorizo around the ribs, then add the liquid from the blender. Cook in the upper half of the oven for 15 minutes.

Without stirring the paella, take a test bite from the side of the pan. If there isn't moisture surrounding the rice, add a few tablespoons of water. Distribute the prawns, clams and mussels around the pan and cook for another 10 minutes, or until the rice has a bit of crunch at the edges but is not undercooked, then serve.

PER SERVING: 310 CALORIES, 18.74G FAT, 12.83G CARBS, 21.11G PROTEIN, 2.81G FIBRE, 89MG CALCIUM, 9.25MG IRON, 696MG SODIUM, 131µG FOLATE

beef and vegetable skewers

Serve these solo or with rice, and don't forget to cook your meat until it's at least medium. If you don't have a gas barbecue, use the grill instead; just don't put the skewers too close to the heat source or they'll burn.

Seves 4

1 tablespoon white rice vinegar
2 tablespoons rapeseed oil
3 garlic cloves, thinly sliced
2 tablespoons plus 1 teaspoon low-sodium soy sauce
2 tablespoons soft dark brown sugar
450g rump steak, cut into 4cm cubes
   (about 24 pieces)
8 closed cup mushrooms, halved
1 red pepper, deseeded and cut into 6cm pieces
1 courgette, cut into 2.5cm-thick rounds
1 aubergine, cut into 2.5cm-thick rounds

Combine the vinegar, oil, garlic, soy sauce and brown sugar in a large resealable plastic bag. Add the beef, seal the bag and leave to marinate, refrigerated, for 2 hours or overnight.

Preheat a gas barbecue or grill. Soak 8 wooden skewers in cold water.

To assemble the skewers, slide a cube of meat, a mushroom half, a piece of red pepper, another cube of meat, a courgette slice, an aubergine slice and another cube of meat onto a skewer. Baste with the marinade. Repeat with all the skewers.

Gently place the skewers on the barbecue grill or grill pan and cook for 8 minutes, or until the meat is just cooked, flipping once and serve.

PER SERVING: 205 CALORIES, 4.10G FAT, 12.43G CARBS, 28.43G PROTEIN, 6.18G FIBRE, 50MG CALCIUM, 2.63MG IRON, 73MG SODIUM, 77µG FOLATE

rosemary and garlic chicken under a brick

This moist, rustic and simple recipe delivers big flavour (and protein) with little guilt, especially if you discard the chicken skin after cooking. Served with blanched veggies tossed in the pan juices, this is a perfect midweek meal.

Serves 4

2 large carrots, peeled and cut into 1cm rounds
2 medium courgettes, cut in half lengthways and sliced
2 x 225g skin-on boneless chicken breasts
1 tablespoon finely chopped rosemary
2 teaspoons finely chopped garlic
sea salt
2 teaspoons olive oil

Bring a large saucepan of water to the boil, then add the carrots and cook for 4 minutes. Add the courgettes, cook for a further 2 minutes, then drain and set aside. Meanwhile, rinse and pat the chicken dry with kitchen paper.

Mix together the rosemary, garlic and 1 teaspoon of salt, and rub it all over the chicken. Heat the oil in a large frying pan over a medium-high heat. Add the chicken, skin-side up. Place a cast-iron or other heavy pan, or brick, that can fit into the pan on top of the chicken, and cook for 6 minutes. Flip the chicken so that it is skin-side down, put the pan or brick back on top and cook for a further 6 minutes. Remove the chicken from the pan and leave to rest.

Add the carrots, courgettes and 1 teaspoon of water to the pan and deglaze while heating and coating the vegetables with the pan juices. Season with salt.

Slice the chicken, divide between 4 serving plates and serve with the courgettes and carrots.

PER SERVING: 247 CALORIES, 11.97G FAT, 7.28G CARBS, 25.27G PROTEIN, 2.18G FIBRE, 42MG CALCIUM, 1.36MG IRON, 687MG SODIUM, 39µG FOLATE

barbecued herb chicken

Here, the fresh, vibrant flavours of the garden brighten up the everyday chicken breast without adding on too many unnecessary calories. Serve it with Barbecued Vegetables (page 116), over Lime Rice with Black Beans and Coriander (page 120), or sliced and layered in a sandwich with lettuce, tomato, mustard and avocado. Don't have a gas barbecue? Bake the chicken at 180°C/350°F/Gas Mark 4 for 20–30 minutes until cooked through.

Serves 4

¼ medium onion, peeled
2 tablespoons rapeseed oil
3 tablespoons freshly squeezed
  lemon juice
1 teaspoon dried oregano
1 teaspoon chopped rosemary
2 fresh sage leaves, chopped
2 heaped tablespoons finely chopped
  flat-leaf parsley
1 teaspoon fresh thyme
½ garlic clove, finely chopped
¾ teaspoon sea salt
pinch of freshly ground black pepper
4 x 175g boneless, skinless
  chicken breasts

Finely grate the onion over a plate, then transfer along with its juice to a food processor or blender. Add all the other ingredients except the chicken and blend until combined.

Transfer to a frying pan and simmer for 5 minutes over a medium heat. Leave to cool. Cover the chicken pieces with the herb mixture and place in a non-reactive container (just large enough to fit) to marinate in the fridge for at least 10 minutes or up to 2 hours.

Preheat a gas barbecue. Place the chicken on the rack away from the direct flame, baste with the marinade and cook for 4–6 minutes. Flip the chicken, baste again and cook for a further 4–6 minutes, or until cooked through. Leave the chicken to rest for 5–10 minutes and then cut into thick slices.

Serve hot or at room temperature.

PER SERVING: 254 CALORIES, 8.20G FAT, 2.37G CARBS, 39.56G PROTEIN, 0.55G FIBRE, 35MG CALCIUM, 1.68MG IRON, 547MG SODIUM, 13µG FOLATE

maple-glazed pork chops with puréed sweet potatoes

Sweet tooths needn't suffer through healthy meals in anticipation of dessert with this dish. Here, protein-rich pork and puréed sweet potatoes (an incredible source of fibre, vitamin B6 and potassium) taste downright decadent thanks to their tangy maple glaze.

Seves 4

4 tablespoons pure maple syrup
2 tablespoons Dijon mustard
2 teaspoons apple cider vinegar
4 x 140–175g boneless pork chops,
   (about 2.5cm thick)
sea salt
2 medium sweet potatoes, peeled
   and cut into 4cm cubes
½ medium onion, peeled (optional)
125ml semi-skimmed milk
freshly ground black pepper
1 teaspoon rapeseed oil

Mix together the maple syrup, mustard and vinegar in a bowl until thoroughly combined. Transfer the mixture to a large resealable plastic bag, add the pork chops and make sure they are well coated. Seal the bag and leave to marinate in the fridge for at least 2 hours or overnight.

Preheat the oven to 190°C/375°F/Gas Mark 5.

Bring a large saucepan of salted water to the boil. Add the sweet potatoes and onion and cook for about 15 minutes until tender. Discard the onion, drain the sweet potatoes in a sieve and leave them until they are dry. Transfer the sweet potatoes to a food processor and purée. Add the milk, ¾ teaspoon of salt and pepper to taste, and keep warm.

Heat the oil in a frying pan until hot but not smoking. Remove the pork chops from the marinade, allowing the excess to drip back into the bag and reserve the marinade. Cook the chops for about 2 minutes on each side until browned, then transfer them to a baking tin. Spoon 1 teaspoon of marinade over each chop and bake for 10–12 minutes, or until just cooked through.

Meanwhile, transfer the reserved marinade to a small saucepan and cook over a low heat for about 7 minutes until reduced and thick and keep warm. To serve, divide the puréed sweet potatoes between 4 serving plates, add a pork chop and drizzle with the maple sauce.

PER SERVING: 305 CALORIES, 5.30G FAT, 28.68G CARBS,35.78G PROTEIN, 2.39G FIBRE, 93MG CALCIUM, 1.50MG IRON, 915MG SODIUM, 8µG FOLATE

comforting pot roast

What's not to love about throwing a bunch of ingredients in a pan, putting it on the hob and returning just in time to devour tender chunks of beef slathered in a rich yet surprisingly wholesome sauce that's stocked with veggies? Adapted from a family recipe shared by talented chef Brett McKee of Oak Steakhouse in Charleston, South Carolina, this vivacious pot roast has staying power because, as McKee promises, a good pot roast gets better and more flavourful as leftovers. Serve it solo or with mashed potatoes, and don't worry about the alcohol content of the included red wine; it evaporates during cooking.

Serves 4

2 teaspoons olive oil
675g joint of silverside or topside beef
sea salt and freshly ground black pepper
2 celery sticks, roughly diced
2 large carrots, peeled and roughly diced
½ large onion, roughly diced
1 medium golden beetroot, peeled
   and roughly diced
1 parsnip, peeled and roughly diced
1 garlic clove, peeled
1½ teaspoons tomato purée
175ml red wine
700ml beef stock
2 tablespoons chopped flat-leaf parsley
1 teaspoon chopped thyme

Heat the olive oil in a flameproof casserole dish or large saucepan until hot but not smoking. Season the beef with salt and pepper, place it in the hot oil and brown it on all sides. Remove and set aside.

Add the celery, carrots, onion, beetroot and parsnip to the pan and cook until they begin to brown. Add the garlic and tomato purée and cook for 1–3 minutes, then add the wine and bring to the boil. Boil for 2 minutes, then add the beef stock, parsley, thyme and beef. Reduce the heat to low and simmer, covered, for 3 hours.

Remove the lid and continue cooking for 30 minutes while the sauce reduces. Season with salt and pepper if you like.

To serve, place a thick slice of the roast on each serving plate and ladle the vegetables and sauce over the meat.

PER SERVING: 380 CALORIES, 8.97G FAT, 17.25G CARBS, 44.92G PROTEIN, 4.04G FIBRE, 94MG CALCIUM, 5.40MG IRON, 1376MG SODIUM, 96µG FOLATE

pasta bolognese

A shortcut to the satisfying Bolognese-style meat sauce in Marcella Hazan's *The Classic Italian Cookbook,* this recipe is a great midweek meal – especially since kids love it too. You can dive into a big bowl with reassurance that it's providing necessary protein. Use wholemeal pasta and you've added fibre to the mix.

Serves 4

1 tablespoon olive oil
225g extra-lean beef mince (less than 9% fat)
125ml dry white wine
60ml milk
250g bottled tomato pasta sauce
sea salt
pinch of ground nutmeg
225g dried spaghetti
freshly grated Parmesan cheese, to serve (optional)

Heat the oil in a medium saucepan over a medium heat. Add the mince and cook, stirring frequently to break it up, for about 5 minutes until it is no longer pink. Add the wine, increase the heat to medium-high and cook for about 10 minutes, stirring occasionally, until it has evaporated. Add the milk and simmer for about 5 minutes, stirring occasionally, until it has evaporated. Add the tomato sauce, ½ teaspoon of salt and the nutmeg, simmer for 5 minutes and keep warm.

Bring a large saucepan of salted water to the boil and cook the spaghetti, according to the packet instructions, until barely al dente. Drain and transfer to 4 serving bowls. Top each with a quarter of the sauce and serve with grated Parmesan, if you like.

PER SERVING: 428 CALORIES, 10.87G FAT, 52.66G CARBS, 20.39G PROTEIN, 3.50G FIBRE, 52MG CALCIUM, 3.71MG IRON, 146µG FOLATE

korean beef broccoli

The Korean-style marinade and super-thin slicing makes the beef tender and flavourful, even when well done. For best results, slice the meat when it's partially frozen and stir-fry until just cooked through. If you're craving spicy food, add some dried chilli flakes to the pan.

Serves 4

450g rump or sirloin steak, thinly sliced
1 heaped tablespoon finely chopped garlic
2 tablespoons grated onion
3 tablespoons soy sauce
1 tablespoon granulated sugar
1 tablespoon runny honey
1 tablespoon sesame oil
1 tablespoon sesame seeds, plus extra to garnish
pinch of freshly ground black pepper
280g broccoli florets, halved lengthways
1 spring onion, sliced into thin strips, to garnish

Combine the beef, garlic, onion, soy sauce, sugar, honey, sesame oil, sesame seeds and pepper in a large resealable plastic bag. Seal the bag and refrigerate for 2–3 hours.

Steam or boil the broccoli until cooked but still firm. Set aside to cool.

Heat a frying pan over a medium-high heat. Add the beef slices, shaking off any marinade, and cook, stirring frequently, for 3–6 minutes or until cooked through. Add the broccoli during the last 2 minutes of cooking, to heat and coat with the cooking juices. If the pan gets too dry, add a little water. Garnish with the spring onion and extra sesame seeds and serve.

PER SERVING: 247 CALORIES, 9.39G FAT, 10.64G CARBS, 28.16G PROTEIN, 0.19G FIBRE, 70MG CALCIUM, 2.81MG IRON, 649MG SODIUM, 67µG FOLATE

pistachio- and herb-crusted rack of lamb with roasted asparagus and rosemary potatoes

This nut-crusted take on famed British chef Gordon Ramsay's herb-crusted rack of lamb, featured on his Channel 4 show 'The F Word', is elegant enough to serve on special occasions and easy enough to prepare on weeknights. Along with style, it provides ample protein from the lamb and fibre from the nuts.

4 small red potatoes, peeled and halved
5 teaspoons extra-virgin olive oil
2 teaspoons chopped fresh rosemary
sea salt and freshly ground black pepper
350g asparagus spears, trimmed
30g finely chopped flat-leaf parsley
1 teaspoon chopped fresh thyme
40g dry-roasted pistachio nuts
2 x 6-rib French-style racks of lamb
   (each rack 350g), trimmed of all
   but a thin layer of fat
1 tablespoon Dijon mustard

Preheat the oven to 200°C/400°F/Gas Mark 6.

Toss the potato halves in 2 teaspoons of the olive oil and 1 teaspoon of the rosemary in a wide bowl to coat. Sprinkle with salt and pepper and then transfer, cut-side down in a single layer, to a baking tray. Roll the asparagus in the same bowl, coating with the remaining oil, then set aside. Roast the potatoes for 35 minutes. Add the asparagus to the baking tray in a single layer and roast for a further 10 minutes; keep warm.

While the potatoes are cooking, blend the parsley, the remaining 1 teaspoon of rosemary and the thyme in a blender or food processor until chopped as finely as possible. Add the pistachios and repeat until the nuts are in the smallest possible pieces. Add 1 teaspoon of the olive oil and blend to combine. Set aside.

Season the lamb with salt and pepper. Heat the remaining 2 teaspoons of olive oil in a large frying pan over a medium-high heat. Sear the meat one rack at a time by cooking the ribs for about 5 minutes until browned, turning once. Transfer the lamb to a large roasting tin, meat-side up, and coat with the mustard.

Gently press the pistachio mixture onto the meaty portion of the rack. Roast the lamb for 20–25 minutes, or until a thermometer inserted diagonally 5cm into its centre (don't touch the bone) registers 68°C/155°F (for medium). Transfer to a chopping board.

Leave to rest for 10 minutes, then gently cut the meat into individual ribs. Serve with the potatoes and asparagus.

PER SERVING: 571 CALORIES, 29.27G FAT, 34.01G CARBS, 39.86G PROTEIN, 6.20G FIBRE, 81MG CALCIUM, 6.95MG IRON, 473MG SODIUM, 123µG FOLATE

bucatini with broad beans and guanciale

World-class flavour plus folate, dietary fibre and protein are yours with this recipe from James Beard Award-winning chef Craig Stoll. The owner of San Francisco's famed Delfina is known for transforming rustic, straightforward Italian cooking into astonishingly good food. Part of his secret is fresh, seasonal ingredients, especially in this case, as the dish is best made late in the growing season when broad beans are starchier. Incidentally, guanciale is cured pig's cheek, similar in texture and flavour to pancetta, which can be substituted in this recipe.

Serves 4–6

85g nitrate-free guanciale or pancetta, diced into 1cm pieces
3 tablespoons extra-virgin olive oil
2 garlic cloves, peeled
sea salt and freshly ground black pepper
1 tablespoon chopped flat-leaf parsley
2.25kg broad beans in the pod, shelled, blanched and peeled
225ml water
450g dried bucatini
3 tablespoons freshly grated Parmesan cheese
freshly grated Pecorino-Romano, to serve

Add the diced guanciale and 2 tablespoons of the olive oil to a heavy-based frying pan. Slowly render the fat from the guanciale until golden and crispy.

Using the side of a sharp knife, smash the garlic and smear it against the chopping board with a pinch of sea salt. Add the smashed garlic to the pan and reduce the heat. Cook slowly until the garlic dissolves into the fat but does not brown. Add the parsley, fry briefly and then add the broad beans and water. Season with salt and pepper. Bring to the boil, then reduce to a simmer. Cook the beans for 15–30 minutes, stirring occasionally, until they begin to break down, depending on the starchiness of the beans. If necessary, add more water.

Bring a large saucepan of salted water to the boil and cook the bucatini, according to the packet instructions, until barely al dente. Drain, reserving 225ml of the pasta water. Return the pasta to the pan and add the broad bean sauce. Add a splash of the reserved pasta water and bring to a simmer. Cook until the sauce reduces and clings to the pasta. Add more pasta water if needed.

Add the Parmesan and remaining 1 tablespoon of olive oil, and season to taste with salt and pepper. Serve sprinkled with some grated Pecorino-Romano and freshly ground black pepper.

PER SERVING: 575 CALORIES, 19.34G FAT, 77.37G CARBS, 20.08G PROTEIN, 2.95G FIBRE, 86MG CALCIUM, 4.03MG IRON, 271MG SODIUM, 291µG FOLATE

bucatini amatriciana with bacon

Iron Chef and supermum Cat Cora kindly customised this – her number-one pregnancy-craving recipe from her cookbook *Classics with a Twist*. She couldn't get enough spiciness, tomatoes and pasta, and once you try this recipe, you may feel the same. When buying ingredients, look for pancetta or guanciale that is nitrate-free; it's healthier for your baby.

Serves 4–6

sea salt
225g nitrate-free smoked pancetta
  or guanciale, thinly sliced and
  finely chopped
1 large onion, halved and sliced
4 garlic cloves, finely chopped
1 teaspoon dried chilli flakes,
  or to taste
250g bottled tomato pasta sauce
250g tinned chopped tomatoes
1 tablespoon chopped oregano
freshly ground black pepper
450g dried bucatini
freshly grated Pecorino-Romano cheese,
  to serve

Bring a large saucepan of salted water to the boil. Line a platter with a piece of kitchen paper, for draining.

Cook the pancetta in a frying pan over a medium heat just until the fat is rendered and the pieces are beginning to crisp. Transfer to the kitchen paper-lined platter.

Pour the fat from the pan, reserving 2 tablespoons. Add the onion and sauté for 5–6 minutes until brown. Add the garlic and chilli flakes and sauté for about 2 minutes, or just until the garlic is lightly browned and aromatic. Add the tomato sauce and the chopped tomatoes. Reduce the heat to low, add the oregano and salt and pepper to taste and simmer for 15–20 minutes until the sauce thickens.

Meanwhile, break the bucatini in half and cook, according to the packet instructions. Drain, reserving 125ml of the pasta water. Return the pasta to the pan and add the sauce. Toss to combine, and add a little of the reserved cooking water if the pasta isn't saucy enough. Sprinkle with freshly grated Pecorino-Romano cheese and serve immediately.

PER SERVING: 480 CALORIES, 16.15G FAT, 64.49G CARBS, 16.77G PROTEIN, 2.46G FIBRE, 71MG CALCIUM, 3.36MG IRON, 225MG SODIUM, 242µG FOLATE

chapter six

sides

braised brussels sprouts with bacon

Forget everything you think about Brussels sprouts – except for, perhaps, that they can cause a little extra flatulence, which is true. This preparation – flavoured with bacon and chicken stock – will make even haters into lovers of these adorable bite-sized heads of cabbage.

Serves 4

12 Brussels sprouts
sea salt
1 thick-cut rasher of nitrate-free bacon, chopped
60ml chicken stock
¼ teaspoon freshly squeezed lemon juice

Trim the ends off the Brussels sprouts and remove and discard any discoloured outer leaves.

Bring a large saucepan of salted water to the boil. Add the sprouts and cook for about 5 minutes until crunchy but tender. Drain, leave to cool and then slice the sprouts in half through the stem.

Cook the bacon in a large frying pan over a medium heat until it begins to brown. Add the sprouts, cut-sides down, in a single layer, and cook for about 4 minutes until browned. Combine the chicken stock and lemon juice in a jug, add them to the pan and cook until the liquid has just evaporated. Serve.

PER SERVING: 40 CALORIES, 1.04G FAT, 5.69G CARBS, 3.05G PROTEIN, 2.17G FIBRE, 24MG CALCIUM, 0.86MG IRON, 81MG SODIUM, 35µG FOLATE

barbecued vegetables

It's easy to forget that sometimes the simplest recipe makes the best food. And these barbecued vegetables are a reason to remember that. Naturally savoury and sweet (due to the caramelising that happens during the cooking process) filling, healthy and exceptionally tasty, they can be served solo, between two slices of bread or diced, tossed and served as a salad.

Serves 4

3 tablespoons olive oil, plus extra for oiling the rack
1 garlic clove, crushed or finely chopped
1 teaspoon sea salt
pinch of freshly ground black pepper
2 courgettes, halved lengthways
1 red pepper, deseeded and quartered
1 orange pepper, deseeded and quartered
1 aubergine, sliced into 1cm disks and salted
5 fresh basil sprigs, to garnish (optional)

Lightly oil a gas barbecue rack and preheat the barbecue.

Mix together the olive oil, garlic, salt and pepper in a bowl. Baste both sides of each vegetable with the garlic olive oil.

Cook the vegetables over a low flame until tender and lightly charred on each side, about 8–10 minutes for the peppers and 8 minutes for the courgette and aubergine. Arrange the vegetables on a platter, garnish with the basil, if you like, and serve warm or at room temperature.

PER SERVING: 157 CALORIES, 10.21 FAT, 14.97G CARBS, 3.21G PROTEIN, 7.02G FIBRE, 32MG CALCIUM, 1.02MG IRON, 595MG SODIUM, 85µG FOLATE

roasted cauliflower with caper vinaigrette

Even if you think you don't like cauliflower, you've got to try this recipe. Absurdly easy to make, it has robust flavour that belies its healthy attributes. In fact, the flavour is so good on its own, you might even want to skip the dressing (and its extra calories). Regardless, you can dine with the confidence that cauliflower is a good source of protein, dietary fibre, vitamins C, K and B6 and folate.

Serves 4

2 tablespoons extra-virgin olive oil
¼ teaspoon sea salt
pinch of freshly ground black pepper
1 cauliflower head (1.1–1.3kg), cut into florets
2 garlic cloves, peeled
1 tablespoon capers, drained and finely chopped
1 teaspoon freshly squeezed lemon juice

Preheat the oven to 230°C/450°F/Gas Mark 8 and place the shelf in the lower third of the oven.

Combine 1 tablespoon of the olive oil, the salt and pepper in a bowl. Add the cauliflower and garlic cloves, and toss until evenly coated. Transfer the mixture to a baking tray and roast for about 25 minutes, turning once, until golden and just tender.

Transfer the cauliflower to a serving bowl and set aside. Transfer the roasted garlic cloves to a small bowl with the capers and mash them together. Whisk in the lemon juice and the remaining 1 tablespoon of olive oil.

Drizzle the dressing over the cauliflower and serve.

PER SERVING: 114 CALORIES, 6.73G FAT, 11.88G CARBS, 4.32G PROTEIN, 5.137G FIBRE, 49MG CALCIUM, 1.04MG IRON, 271MG SODIUM, 119µG FOLATE

creamed swiss chard

Anyone who loves creamed spinach will be smitten with this creamy dish, rich with vitamins, minerals and daily fibre. You can make it up to a day ahead and refrigerate it until you are ready to serve.

Serves 4

2 teaspoons extra-virgin olive oil
1 medium onion, chopped
225g Swiss chard leaves, chopped
75ml water
125ml semi-skimmed milk
1 tablespoon plain flour
generous pinch of ground nutmeg
½ teaspoon sea salt
freshly ground black pepper

Heat the olive oil in a large saucepan over a medium heat. Add the onion and cook for 3–4 minutes until translucent but not browned. Add the chard and water and cook for 4 minutes, covered but stirring occasionally, until tender.

Heat the milk in a small saucepan over a medium heat until hot, then whisk in the flour and nutmeg until blended. Cook, stirring, for 3–5 minutes until the sauce thickens. Pour the milk mixture into the Swiss chard, add the salt and pepper to taste and stir. Serve immediately.

PER SERVING: 161 CALORIES, 3.45G FAT, 24.53G CARBS, 5.25G PROTEIN, 4.17G FIBRE, 59MG CALCIUM, 3.14MG IRON, 309MG SODIUM, 81µG FOLATE

sautéed spinach with garlic and lemon

A lighter, cleaner-flavoured alternative to the comforting Creamed Swiss Chard (page 119), this ultra-healthy side dish is a perfect accompaniment to grilled meats, including Barbecued Herbed Chicken (page 102).

Serves 4

2 teaspoons extra-virgin olive oil
½ teaspoon finely chopped garlic
280g baby spinach leaves
sea salt
4 lemon wedges

Heat the oil in a large frying pan over a medium heat. Add the garlic and sauté for about 1 minute until pale golden. Add the spinach and cook, stirring occasionally, for about 3 minutes, or until wilted.

Season to taste with salt and serve with the lemon wedges on the side.

PER SERVING: 58 CALORIES, 2.51G FAT, 14.24G CARBS, 3.34G PROTEIN, 6.64G FIBRE, 136MG CALCIUM, 2.70MG IRON, 640MG SODIUM, 137µG FOLATE

lime rice with black beans and coriander

A gorgeous accompaniment to barbecued chicken or fish, or the perfect base for a bowl of barbecued or grilled steak, chopped Cos lettuce and salsa. This pretty and lively side dish transforms everyday rice into tangy, exciting goodness. It also provides a decent dose of protein, folate and dietary fibre.

Serves 4

380g tinned black beans
1 teaspoon vegetable oil
1 teaspoon butter
½ teaspoon finely chopped garlic
125g basmati rice
225ml water
½ teaspoon sea salt
1 tablespoon freshly squeezed lime juice
⅛ teaspoon finely grated lime zest
1 tablespoon chopped coriander

Drain, rinse and strain the black beans to remove the excess moisture. Set aside.

Heat the oil and butter in a large heavy saucepan over a low heat until hot but not smoking. Stir in the garlic and sauté for 2 minutes, stirring frequently. Stir in the rice. Add the water, salt and lime juice and zest and bring to the boil, then cover and simmer over a low heat for 20 minutes.

Fluff up the rice with a fork, and gently mix in the coriander and black beans. Serve.

PER SERVING: 216 CALORIES, 2.45G FAT, 40.39G CARBS, 7.97G PROTEIN, 6.04G FIBRE, 28MG CALCIUM, 2.70MG IRON, 447MG SODIUM, 167µG FOLATE

oven-roasted parmesan french fries

These delightfully crispy, Parmesan-sprinkled, oven-roasted potatoes are almost as satisfying as their deep-fried friends – especially when dipped into your favourite condiment. After all, what are French fries but gorgeously greasy vehicles for ketchup, aioli or gravy? Make these to satisfy your craving for fries and you'll feel a little less guilty when you reach for seconds. And if you're a real traditionalist, skip the cheese.

Serves 4

4 large unpeeled Russet (or other starchy) potatoes, washed, dried and sliced into 1cm wedges
1 tablespoon plus 1½ teaspoons rapeseed oil
1 teaspoon sea salt
3 tablespoons freshly grated Parmesan cheese

Preheat the oven to 230°C/450°F/Gas Mark 8. Line a baking sheet with baking parchment.

Toss the potato wedges in the oil in a large bowl until well coated. Spread the potatoes in a single layer on the lined baking sheet and sprinkle with the salt. Roast for 15 minutes. Turn the wedges over and continue roasting until browned and crisp.

Remove from the oven, toss in a bowl with the Parmesan and serve hot or at room temperature.

PER SERVING: 376 CALORIES, 7.75G FAT, 64.45G CARBS, 11.68G PROTEIN, 6.88G FIBRE, 180MG CALCIUM, 3.32MG IRON, 794MG SODIUM, 78μG FOLATE

chinese-style green beans

Sometimes called 'dry-braised', these stir-fried beans have such robust flavour – thanks to the ginger, garlic and soy sauce – that they make a deeply satisfying meal, especially if paired with a little rice. Want to add extra kick? Throw some chilli paste or dried chilli flakes into the mix during cooking.

Serves 4

2 teaspoons vegetable oil
450g green beans or Chinese long beans, trimmed
1 tablespoon chopped garlic
1 tablespoon peeled and chopped fresh ginger
2 medium spring onions, white and green parts, finely chopped
1 tablespoon soy sauce

Heat 1 teaspoon of the oil in a wok or large sauté pan over a medium-high heat. Add the beans and stir-fry, stirring frequently, for about 7 minutes until they start to shrivel and brown.

Transfer the beans to a kitchen paper-lined plate. Increase the heat to high and add the remaining 1 teaspoon of oil, the garlic, ginger and spring onions to the pan. Stir-fry for a few seconds.

Add the green beans and the soy sauce, stir and serve warm.

PER SERVING: 63 CALORIES, 2.35G FAT, 9.76G CARBS, 2.81G PROTEIN, 4.13G FIBRE, 50MG CALCIUM, 1.42MG IRON, 259MG SODIUM, 46µG FOLATE

quinoa tabbouleh

This spin on the classic Middle Eastern salad swaps traditionally used bulgar wheat (which you could also use) for nutritional superstar quinoa, which is high in 'complete protein', meaning that it includes all nine essential amino acids. Serve it as a dinner side dish or store it, covered, in the fridge for a healthy and filling snack.

Serves 4

1 tablespoon extra-virgin olive oil
60ml freshly squeezed lemon juice
½ teaspoon sea salt
pinch of freshly ground pepper
370g cooked quinoa
90g deseeded and finely diced tomatoes
70g peeled and diced cucumber
60g finely chopped flat-leaf parsley
4 medium spring onions, white and green parts, finely chopped
3 tablespoons thinly sliced mint leaves, plus whole leaves to garnish

Combine the olive oil, lemon juice, salt and pepper in a small bowl. Set aside.

Toss together the quinoa, tomatoes, cucumber, parsley, spring onions and mint in a serving bowl. Add the dressing, toss until evenly coated and serve.

PER SERVING: 161 CALORIES, 3.45G FAT, 24.53G CARBS, 5.25G PROTEIN, 4.17G FIBRE, 59MG CALCIUM, 3.14MG IRON, 309MG SODIUM, 81µG FOLATE

chapter seven
desserts & beverages

baked apple à la mode

You can treat yourself to a sizeable dessert while only putting a small dent in the ice cream tub if you partake in this heaven-scented baked dessert. Or skip the ice cream altogether and you've got a great breakfast.

Serves 4

2 large Golden Delicious apples, halved and cored
60ml apple juice
1 teaspoon freshly squeezed lemon juice
¼ teaspoon vanilla extract
⅓ teaspoon ground cinnamon
1 heaped tablespoon raisins (optional)
150g vanilla ice cream
2 tablespoons granola (see page 32, or shop-bought)

Preheat the oven to 160°C/325°F/Gas Mark 3.

Place the apples, cut-sides down, in a baking dish just large enough to contain them.

Combine the apple juice, lemon juice, vanilla extract and cinnamon in a bowl, and then pour the mixture around the apples. Bake the apples for about 20 minutes, occasionally basting, until they are soft. Leave to cool slightly.

Spoon one apple half, a quarter of the ice cream and ½ tablespoon of granola into each serving dish and serve immediately.

PER SERVING: 140 CALORIES, 2.67G FAT, 28.93G CARBS, 1.68G PROTEIN, 3.48G FIBRE, 35MG CALCIUM, 0.47MG IRON, 16MG SODIUM, 7µG FOLATE

banana 'ice cream' with caramel and toasted walnuts

Believe it or not, you can have your ice cream and eat it too – if you use this surprising recipe, which miraculously transforms your basic banana (loaded with fibre, vitamins C and B6, potassium and manganese) into gelato-like decadence. Seriously. With hardly a hint of sugar, eggs or cream in the 'ice cream', you can guiltlessly add a sprinkle of toasted shredded coconut or a drizzle of chocolate or caramel without indulging in too many empty calories. There's no need to hold back on the toasted walnuts, either; they're an excellent source of omega-3 fatty acids.

Serves 4

4 frozen peeled bananas
4 tablespoons toasted or raw walnuts
4 teaspoons shop-bought chocolate or caramel sauce

Slice the bananas into 1cm-thick discs. Put them in a blender on the slowest speed until they separate into little bits. Stop and scrape down the side. Repeat several times until the banana begins to form into a creamy, gelato-like ball. Blend until smooth.

Spoon the mixture into 4 dessert bowls and top each with a tablespoon of walnuts and drizzle over a little sauce.

PER SERVING: 174 CALORIES, 5.32G FAT, 31.94G CARBS, 2.69G PROTEIN, 3.74G FIBRE, 14MG CALCIUM, 0.60MG IRON, 22MG SODIUM, 30µG FOLATE

banana coconut cream crumbles

Crunchy on top, smooth and creamy in the middle and lighter than it looks and tastes, this glorious dessert is a fine source of dietary fibre, vitamins B6 and C and potassium. It's also elegant enough to impress company with minimal effort.

Serves 4

30g caster sugar
1½ tablespoons cornflour
⅓ teaspoon sea salt
125ml semi-skimmed milk
175ml reduced-fat coconut milk
½ large egg
½ teaspoon vanilla extract
35g plain flour
35g whole blanched almonds, ground into a coarse flour
   in a coffee grinder or food processor
50g soft light brown sugar
30g unsalted butter, cut into 1cm pieces
2 ripe bananas

Whisk together the caster sugar, cornflour and ¼ teaspoon of the salt in a small bowl.

Bring the milk and coconut milk to a simmer in a heavy, medium-sized saucepan. Gradually add the sugar mixture, stirring constantly, then whisk in the egg. Cook, stirring, over a medium heat for about 5 minutes until the mixture boils and thickens. Remove from the heat, mix in the vanilla extract and set aside.

Put the flour, ground almonds, brown sugar, the remaining salt and the butter in a bowl and mix until the butter becomes the size of small peas. Set aside.

Preheat the grill. Slice the banana thinly (5mm-thick) and layer into the bases of 4 flameproof ramekins. Next, add a layer of coconut cream mixture, dividing it evenly between the ramekins. Then crumble over the butter-almond topping mixture so that it covers the top entirely. Place the ramekins on a baking tray and cook under the grill for about 3 minutes, or until the crumble tops are golden brown. Serve immediately.

PER SERVING: 329 CALORIES, 16.77G FAT, 42.60G CARBS, 5.32G PROTEIN, 2.58G FIBRE, 85 MG CALCIUM, 2.18MG IRON, 250MG SODIUM, 24µG FOLATE

raspberry turnovers

As decadent as turnovers found in your favourite bakery – complete with gooey fruit filling wrapped in a flaky, buttery crust – these homemade versions use less puff pastry and provide fewer calories without losing any of the flavour. Plus, raspberries include great dietary fibre, vitamin C and manganese.

Serves 4

butter, for greasing
250g fresh raspberries
4½ teaspoons caster sugar
1 tablespoon water
2 teaspoons freshly squeezed lemon juice
1½ teaspoons cornflour
4 x 7.5cm squares of chilled, ready-rolled puff pastry

Preheat the oven to 200°C/400°F/Gas Mark 6. Grease a baking tray with butter.

Place the berries, 4 teaspoons of the sugar and the water in a saucepan over a medium heat and cook, stirring frequently, until the berries break down. Add the lemon juice and cornflour and cook, stirring, for about 3 minutes until the berry mixture thickens. Set aside.

Roll out each piece of puff pastry to 10cm square and place them on the prepared baking tray. Place a quarter of the raspberry mixture in the centre, leaving 2cm of dough on each side. Using a pastry brush, dampen the dough with water. Fold the dough in half diagonally over the filling. Press the edges to seal and crimp them with a fork. Brush the top of each turnover with water and sprinkle evenly with the remaining sugar. Chill in the fridge for 20–30 minutes.

With the tip of a paring knife, cut 3 small slits in the top of each pastry. Bake in the centre of the oven for 15 minutes, or until the pastry is golden. Serve warm.

PER SERVING: 210 CALORIES, 10.53G FAT, 25.99G CARBS, 2.82G PROTEIN, 4.44G FIBRE, 18MG CALCIUM, 1.16MG IRON, 71MG SODIUM, 35µG FOLATE

aniseed-kissed blueberry and almond clafoutis

A clafoutis is a pancake-custard hybrid made of fruit and a cake mixture. In this case, the result is an antioxidant-rich blueberry bonanza surrounded by a thin but deliciously dense and creamy layer of cake. Don't be afraid to substitute other fruits – pear or plum slices or cherry halves would also be excellent. And if you're concerned with over-eating, you can bake the berries and cake mixture in cupcake trays (just be sure to cook them for a shorter time). Finally, use organic blueberries; their non-organic counterparts are one of the highest pesticide-contaminated fruits on the market.

Serves 6

75g whole blanched almonds
225ml semi-skimmed milk
¾ teaspoon butter, for greasing
150g fresh or frozen organic blueberries
2 large eggs, at room temperature
1 teaspoon almond extract
1 teaspoon aniseed-flavoured liqueur
¼ teaspoon sea salt
60g caster sugar
6 tablespoons plain flour
25g flaked almonds
½ teaspoon icing sugar

Process the whole almonds in a food processor until finely ground; do not overprocess or they will become mushy. Transfer to a small saucepan, add the milk and bring it to a simmer. Remove the almond milk from the heat and leave to stand for 30 minutes.

Pour the milk through a fine-mesh sieve, pressing the almond bits to extract all the liquid. Discard the solids and set aside.

Preheat the oven to 190°C/375°F/Gas Mark 5. Grease a 20cm baking tin with the butter and scatter the berries along the base.

Whisk the eggs, almond extract, liqueur, salt and caster sugar in a bowl until well blended. Add the almond milk and whisk to blend. Sift the flour into the mixture and beat until smooth. Pour the mixture over the blueberries in the baking tin, top with the flaked almonds and bake for about 30 minutes until set and a knife inserted into the centre comes out clean.

Leave to cool, dust with the icing sugar and serve warm or at room temperature.

PER SERVING: 226 CALORIES, 9.67G FAT, 26.96G CARBS, 7.81G PROTEIN, 2.72G FIBRE, 101MG CALCIUM, 1.07MG IRON, 138MG SODIUM, 20µG FOLATE

angel food cake with pineapple compôte

A blend of the light lusciousness of angel food cake and the moist, sweet-tangy goodness of pineapple upside-down cake, this recipe allows you to feel like you're really indulging – without going too far down a decadent path. Incidentally, you can swap the pineapple for strawberries or peaches or both (with orange-zest strands, as shown opposite), or skip fruit altogether and add two teaspoons of grated lime, orange or lemon zest to infuse a citrus flavour into the cake. Bonus: you can freeze any extra cake in clingfilm-wrapped single servings (keep the pineapple separate) for future cravings.

Serves 12

12 large egg whites
1 teaspoon vanilla extract
1 teaspoon cream of tartar
140g caster sugar
100g plain flour, sifted
¼ teaspoon plus a pinch of sea salt
15g butter
100g soft light brown sugar
250g tinned pineapple chunks in
  natural juice, strained and finely chopped

Position a shelf in the centre of the oven. Preheat the oven to 180°C/350°F/Gas Mark 4.

Beat the egg whites and vanilla in a large bowl with a hand-held electric whisk until frothy. Add the cream of tartar and beat at high speed until soft peaks form. Gradually add the caster sugar, again beating until stiff peaks form.

Mix together the flour and salt in a small bowl. Sprinkle one-third of the flour mixture over the egg whites and gently fold in until incorporated. Repeat with the remaining flour mixture, a third at a time. Gently spoon the mixture into an ungreased angel food cake tin (with a hole in the middle). Bake for 35 minutes, or until the cake is springy to the touch and a skewer comes out clean when you insert it into the centre. Leave the cake to cool upside down on a wire rack for 1 hour or more.

Meanwhile, put the butter and brown sugar in a small saucepan over a medium heat and stir until the butter melts. Add the pineapple and a generous pinch of sea salt. Set aside.

Gently remove the cake from the pan, slice it, then serve with a heaped tablespoon of the pineapple compôte.

PER SERVING: 136 CALORIES, 0.95G FAT, 28.05G CARBS, 4.11G PROTEIN, 0.36G FIBRE, 11MG CALCIUM, 0.75MG IRON, 100MG SODIUM, 17µG FOLATE

chocolate coconut oatmeal cookies

Moist yet crisp on the edges, these cookies promise cholesterol-fighting fibre, folic acid and essential fatty acids – not to mention exceptional flavour. Add dried currants, cranberries or raisins, or almond or pecan bits for even more pizzazz.

Makes 24 cookies

115g unsalted butter, at room temperature
90g soft dark brown sugar
1 large egg, at room temperature
1 teaspoon vanilla extract
100g plain flour
½ teaspoon baking powder
½ teaspoon ground cinnamon
½ teaspoon sea salt
45g desiccated coconut
120g rolled (porridge) oats
45g dark chocolate chips

Preheat the oven to 180°C/350°F/Gas Mark 4. Line a baking tray with baking parchment.

Beat together the butter and sugar in a large bowl until fluffy. Mix in the egg and vanilla extract until well combined.

Sift the flour, baking powder, cinnamon and salt together into a separate bowl, and fold into the butter mixture. Mix in the coconut, oats and chocolate chips until just combined.

Drop heaped tablespoons of the mixture, 2.5cm apart, onto the baking tray (or use a piping bag to make the more traditional swirl-shaped cookies). Bake for 15 minutes until golden. Leave to cool completely before serving.

PER COOKIE: 120 CALORIES, 5.55G FAT, 14.64G CARBS, 2.53G PROTEIN, 1.37G FIBRE, 17MG CALCIUM, 0.68MG IRON, 68MG SODIUM, 8µG FOLATE

ultra-chocolatey meringue cookies

Crisp melt-in-your-mouth texture, rich brownie-like flavour and an astoundingly low calorie count make these light-as-air, two-bite cookies a nearly perfect partner for the pregnant chocoholic. The fact that egg whites are a solid source of protein seals the deal. Tip: to avoid eating them all in one sitting, store extra cookies in a container for up to two months.

Makes approximately 30 cookies

3 medium egg whites
⅛ teaspoon sea salt
⅛ teaspoon cream of tartar
½ teaspoon vanilla extract (or peppermint extract)
60g caster sugar
20g cocoa powder

Preheat the oven to 110°C/225°F/Gas Mark ¼. Line 2 baking trays with foil.

Beat together the egg whites, salt, cream of tartar and vanilla in a large glass bowl until soft peaks form. Gradually add the sugar, beating until just stiff again. Sift in the cocoa powder, then gently fold in until incorporated.

Drop heaped teaspoonfuls of the mixture, 2.5cm apart, onto the baking trays. Bake for 1¾ hours. Leave to cool completely. Store the cookies in a cool, dry place.

PER COOKIE: 12 CALORIES, 0.09G FAT, 2.68G CARBS, 0.50G PROTEIN, 0.24G FIBRE, 1MG CALCIUM, 0.10MG IRON, 15MG SODIUM, 0µG FOLATE

watermelon-yogurt granita

Watermelon is not only refreshing, it's also a favourite fruit for fighting morning sickness, and a natural diuretic, which means it battles bloatedness. Plus, it tastes great.

Serves 4

900g watermelon flesh, cut into 2.5cm chunks and chilled, plus 4 small watermelon wedges
3 tablespoons caster sugar
60ml freshly squeezed lemon juice
490g low-fat or fat-free Greek yogurt

Purée the watermelon chunks in a food processor or blender with the sugar, lemon juice and yogurt. Pour into a shallow container and freeze for 1 hour.

Using a fork, stir the granita, breaking up any stubborn solid parts. Freeze again for about 2–3 hours until firm, scraping the mixture with a fork every 30 minutes to form ice crystals.

Transfer to 4 dessert bowls, garnish with a watermelon wedge and serve.

PER SERVING: 262 CALORIES, 0.74G FAT, 58.90G CARBS, 10.21G PROTEIN, 2.12G FIBRE, 280MG CALCIUM, 1.35MG IRON, 99MG SODIUM, 31µG FOLATE

lemon rosemary ice lollies

In aromatherapy, rosemary is used to battle fatigue and this refreshing recipe uses it to perk up both the spirit and the palate. Meanwhile, the tang of lemon quells the very common craving for citrus, and the ice-cold nature of an ice lolly cools down the over-heated pregnant body.

Makes 8

475ml water
3 x 10cm fresh rosemary sprigs
50g caster sugar
125ml freshly squeezed lemon juice

Combine the water and rosemary in a medium saucepan and bring to a simmer, stirring occasionally. Remove from the heat, add the sugar and stir until it has dissolved. Cover and leave the ingredients to infuse for 10 minutes.

Add the lemon juice, stir and strain into ice-lolly moulds. Freeze for 2–3 hours until completely frozen. Enjoy!

PER POP: 28 CALORIES, 0.03G FAT, 7.70G CARBS, 0.08G PROTEIN, 0.15G FIBRE, 4MG CALCIUM, 1.07MG IRON, 2MG SODIUM, 20µG FOLATE

strawberry-rhubarb ice lollies

The sweet-sour combination of strawberry and rhubarb is frequently used in baked, crumble-topped desserts. But this version, based on a recipe by Massachusetts chef Jason Brown, moves the tangy, complementary flavours into fantastic frozen-dessert territory – with less fat and fewer calories but just as much calcium, dietary fibre and vitamin C. Note: you may need to use more or less sugar depending on the ripeness of the strawberries.

Makes 6

4 rhubarb stalks, cut into 1cm pieces
350ml water
60g caster sugar
280g fresh organic strawberries, hulled and halved
2 tablespoons freshly squeezed lemon juice
pinch of sea salt

Combine the rhubarb, water, sugar and strawberries in a large saucepan and simmer, stirring frequently, for about 20 minutes until the rhubarb is extra-soft. Add the lemon juice and salt, transfer the mixture to a blender and purée. Leave to cool.

Pour the mixture into ice-lolly moulds and freeze for at least 2 hours.

PER SERVING: 70 CALORIES, 0.19G FAT, 17.66G CARBS, 0.72G PROTEIN, 1.82G FIBRE, 40MG CALCIUM, 0.32MG IRON, 52MG SODIUM, 17µG FOLATE

peanut butter-banana chocolate shake

A dessert and mini-meal, this rich, decadent drink by mum and athlete Jill Jackson tastes as good as it sounds and provides protein, dietary fibre and vitamin B6.

Serves 1

½ banana, peeled and frozen
125ml skimmed milk
2 tablespoons peanut butter
1 tablespoon chocolate syrup

Combine all the ingredients in a blender and blend until smooth. Pour into a glass and enjoy.

PER SERVING: 333 CALORIES, 16.02G FAT, 38.02G CARBS, 13.19G PROTEIN, 3.94G FIBRE, 170MG CALCIUM, 1.18MG IRON, 210MG SODIUM, 40µG FOLATE

blueberry-mango smoothie

Greek yogurt adds protein to this exceptionally delicious start to the day.

Serves 1

125ml apple juice
85g fresh or frozen mango flesh, cut into small pieces
½ fresh or frozen banana
20g fresh or frozen organic blueberries
60g low-fat natural yogurt
1 teaspoon runny honey

Combine all the ingredients in a blender and blend until smooth. Pour into a glass and enjoy.

PER SERVING: 227 CALORIES, 0.54G FAT, 54.72G CARBS, 4.86G PROTEIN, 3.73G FIBRE, 141MG CALCIUM, 0.55MG IRON, 52MG SODIUM, 30µG FOLATE

warm vanilla milk

Whether you're in need of a soothing late-night snack or something to warm your soul, this gourmet version of a childhood favourite does the trick while providing you with vitamin D, riboflavin and calcium. Plus, cinnamon is said to help with indigestion and nausea.

Serves 1

225ml semi-skimmed milk
1 teaspoon vanilla extract
2 teaspoons runny honey
pinch of ground cinnamon

Stir together the milk, vanilla, honey and cinnamon in a small saucepan over a medium heat. Heat until just hot and serve warm.

PER SERVING: 172 CALORIES, 2.73G FAT, 26.01G CARBS, 9.73G PROTEIN, 0.20G FIBRE, 352MG CALCIUM, 0.24MG IRON, 142MG SODIUM, 14µG FOLATE

citrus slushy

While a serious citrus craving may never be wholly satisfied, it can be temporarily abated with this cooling combo of frozen grapefruit and orange juice. Bonus: it delivers a nice dose of vitamin C. Tip: make extra citrus ice cubes, keep them frozen and whip up a slushy whenever you get the urge.

Serves 1

125ml freshly squeezed grapefruit juice
125ml freshly squeezed orange juice
2 teaspoons caster sugar, or extra to taste, depending on the ripeness of the fruit
125ml water

Combine all the ingredients in a bowl and stir until the sugar dissolves. Transfer to an ice-cube tray and freeze for 1–2 hours until frozen.

Place the frozen cubes in a blender with the water and blend until slushy, adding a little more water if necessary. Pour into a glass and drink with a straw for added fun.

PER SERVING: 135 CALORIES, 0.19G FAT, 32.66G CARBS, 1.49G PROTEIN, 0.37G FIBRE, 24MG CALCIUM, 0.50MG IRON, 2MG SODIUM, 49µG FOLATE

ginger limeade

Frequently served hot or cold in the spas of Bali, Indonesia, this soothing concoction works wonders for morning sickness and gastro-intestinal stress (thanks to the fresh ginger). It also tastes so good that you may want to remember the recipe for post-baby cocktail parties – adding white rum instantly transforms it into a sexy cocktail.

Serves 1

1 piece of fresh ginger about the size of a plum tomato, peeled
120ml water
40g runny honey
125ml freshly squeezed lime juice

Grate the ginger on the finest holes of a box grater over a plate. Transfer all of the grated ginger (including from inside the grater) and ginger juice to a small saucepan. Add the water and bring to the boil.

Remove from the heat, stir in the honey until dissolved, and let cool. Pour the sweetened ginger juice through a fine-mesh strainer, pressing the pulp to squeeze out all the liquid. Discard the pulp. Add the lime juice to the ginger juice, stir until combined, and serve over ice.

PER SERVING: 44 CALORIES, 0.04G FAT, 12.34G CARBS, 0.27G PROTEIN, 0.26G FIBRE, 5MG CALCIUM, 0.11MG IRON, 1MG SODIUM, 3µG FOLATE,

spa water

When pregnant, little things you can do to pamper yourself can really brighten your day. This recipe is a case in point. An easy way to add subtle flavour, flair and visual elegance to everyday water, it captures the soothing, luxurious sentiment of a day spa.

Serves 6–8

½ lemon
½ lime
½ cucumber, peeled and sliced
a bunch of mint, bruised slightly to release the flavour

Slice the lemon and lime into thin wheels and transfer to a jug. Add the cucumber and mint.

Fill the jug with filtered water and refrigerate for at least 2 hours to let the flavours infuse. Enjoy.

PER SERVING: 8 CALORIES, 0.06G FAT, 2.31G CARBS, 0.46G PROTEIN, 1.08G FIBRE, 21MG CALCIUM, 0.90MG IRON, 2MG SODIUM, 9µG FOLATE

tropical tease

You can forget ho-hum virgin options if you serve this drink at your next party. The exotic flavours of ginger, mango and pomegranate enlivened with bubbly water turn the virgin cocktail into a celebratory affair. Plus you can easily add a shot of vodka or rum to each drink for those who are not expecting.

Serves 1

3 fresh mint leaves
1 teaspoon-size piece of fresh ginger, peeled
3 tablespoons pomegranate concentrate
3 tablespoons mango juice
1 teaspoon fresh lemon juice
110ml tonic

Muddle the mint leaves with the ginger in a tall cocktail glass to infuse their flavours. Add the pomegranate concentrate, mango juice and lemon juice, and stir to combine.

Fill the glass with ice, top with tonic and serve.

PER SERVING: 58 CALORIES, 0.22G FAT, 14.54G CARBS, 0.74G PROTEIN, 1.41G FIBRE, 52MG CALCIUM, 2.27MG IRON, 35MG SODIUM, 31µG FOLATE

watermelon mamarita

Just because you're steering clear of alcohol doesn't mean you can't raise a glass in celebration and this virgin rendition of a watermelon margarita gives you a very good reason to toast. Created by award-winning bartender Jeff Burkhart, it has all the festivity of happy hour, minus the hangover – and it's made from watermelon, which is a natural diuretic and morning-sickness helper. Cheers!

Serves 1

1 large wedge fresh watermelon, deseeded and chopped
2 tablespoons fresh lemon juice
juice of ½ lime, plus 1 lime wedge
1 tablespoon agave nectar or honey

Fill a serving glass with ice, then transfer to a blender. Add the watermelon, lemon juice and lime juice and blend. While blending, add the agave nectar and continue blending until smooth.

Taste – you may need to adjust the lime juice, agave or both. Pour the mamarita back into the serving glass, garnish with the lime wedge and serve.

PER SERVING: 119 CALORIES, 0.16G FAT, 33.19G CARBS, 1.19G PROTEIN, 1.04G FIBRE, 16MG CALCIUM, 0.51MG IRON, 1MG SODIUM

mother mary

The genius behind the virgin Bloody Mary is that it can double as a mocktail and a wholesome drinkable meal – all the while imparting your body with ample amounts of vitamins A, C and B6, folate and potassium.

Serves 1

110ml tomato juice
1 teaspoon fresh lemon juice
½ teaspoon Worcestershire sauce
½ teaspoon prepared horseradish, or more to taste
2 drops Tabasco sauce
freshly ground black pepper
1 celery stalk
1 long, thin carrot stick

In a bowl or cocktail shaker, combine the tomato juice, lemon juice, Worcestershire sauce, horseradish and Tabasco and mix well. Add pepper to taste.

Fill a tall glass with ice, pour your Mary over the ice and garnish with the celery and carrot.

PER SERVING: 28 CALORIES, 0.15G FAT, 7.34G CARBS, 1.21G PROTEIN, 1.08G FIBRE, 24MG CALCIUM, 0.82MG IRON, 122MG SODIUM, 30µG FOLATE

index